D1591278

AMAZULU.

THE ZULUS,

THEIR

Past History, Manners, Customs, and Language,

WITH OBSERVATIONS ON

THE COUNTRY AND ITS PRODUCTIONS, CLIMATE, ETC., THE ZULU WAR, AND ZULULAND SINCE THE WAR.

BY

THOMAS B. JENKINSON, B.A.,

S.P.G., NATAL, 1873–1879, LATE CANON OF MARITZBURG.

NEGRO UNIVERSITIES PRESS
NEW YORK

Originally published in 1882
by W. H. Allen & Co., London

Reprinted 1969 by
Negro Universities Press
A DIVISION OF GREENWOOD PUBLISHING CORP.
NEW YORK

SBN 8371-1726-7

PRINTED IN UNITED STATES OF AMERICA

INTRODUCTION.

As Ketchwayo, late Chief-paramount of the Zulu nation, is on his way to England, many will be glad to have more information about him and his case.

I was bidding farewell to my friends in England before leaving for Natal as Missionary of the Society for the Propagation of the Gospel, when tidings came of the death of Panda, or Umpande, supreme chief of Zululand, and father of Ketchwayo. I sailed for Port Natal on 5th March 1873, stayed in that country above six years, and landed at Plymouth in July 1879, just as the news came of the decisive battle of Ulundi, which completed the overthrow of the Zulu army. I was in Natal during the six months of the Zulu War.

As it was part of my duty to learn all about the natives, and to study the language, manners, and customs, and as I had access to the library of Dr. Callaway (now Bishop of Kaffraria), it may be supposed that I formed a fair acquaintance with the Zulu question. I can well remember what we felt about the Zulus and their chief, years before the war broke out. Fully one year before it did break out, I wrote to the S. P. G. in London, anticipating the war, and imploring aid from home in our defence, for that, sooner or later, the torrent pent up in Zululand must burst forth. Twice before it had burst upon Natal, carrying destruction before it—once in Chaka's time, and again in Dingaan's. Years before it broke out, I was in Pietermaritzburg, and heard that the 1–13th Regiment P.A.L.I., under Colonel Montgomery, had gone up the country towards the Transvaal. I at once remarked, " I hope they won't come back until they have taken over the Zulu country."

I met Dr. Sutherland in Maritzburg about the same time, and he told me that news had come from the agent in Zululand to the effect that young Zulu was thirsting for blood, and, like bloodhounds in a leash, could scarcely be restrained. In our neighbourhood (fifty miles south of Maritzburg) it was quite a common thing for the natives to chaff the white men, and to threaten them with Ketchwayo, saying that the day was coming when "all the white men would be driven into the sea." This sort of talk arose, not so much from the disaffection of the Natal natives as from the knowledge they had of what was brewing in the land whence they had fled for refuge into Natal; for it is a most significant fact—which our rulers would do well to consider—that ever since the time that Captain Allen Gardiner visited Dingaan and obtained a sort of grant of Natal for the British in 1835, refugees, fleeing from cruel oppression, have been constantly coming into Natal, and so under British rule. A vote of the Zulus, if taken, should include the Zulus in Natal.

My own opinions were recorded daily at the time and in the country, surrounded as I was by thousands of Zulus, and with no white man within five miles. My son-in-law, daughter, and only son, living in Zululand, have told the rest of the story.

It is now my deliberate conviction that the overthrow of the Zulu power, though a terrible thing at the time, was a blessing to the whole of the Zulu nation (estimated at about 750,000 people) dwelling in Zululand and Natal. What say others competent to judge?

Dr. Emile Holub, a traveller and a foreigner, living in the Cape Colony, and the author of a work on South Africa, writes as follows :—" A great mistake is made if any one of us thinks that the danger in store is only for those living in Natal and the Transvaal. We must look upon the matter just as if we were insulted and attacked ourselves. The Zulu crater throws its fire high over the whole of South Africa ; the lava spreads over all its countries, Zululand being the concentration of *all* the native dissatisfaction. All those tribes who seek their welfare by overwhelming the race of the whites, look with true desire towards this volcano, sigh in thought and word, and secretly send messengers into Cetywayo's laager. There the last outburst of all the lowest savage vices seeks its protection, finds its nursery, and hopes for its salvation."

The following is taken from a letter by the Big-

garsberg Correspondent to the "Natal Mercury":
"It is a fact, known to all the border residents
both in Natal and the Transvaal, that the Zulus
have been preparing for war for the past three
years. The Zulus insulted British authority. The
administrator at the Blood river was openly insulted, and nearly shot. Envoys on a message to
the Zulu King were forced to witness a review of
the Zulu army, and were insulted and challenged.
At the sitting of the Commission at Rorke's Drift,
British officers and authority were again insulted,
and defiance hurled at them again and again. The
Zulus were determined to be avenged upon Natal for
sheltering refugees—both men, women and children.
When the missionaries and traders were forced to
leave Zululand towards the end of last year (1878),
they knew the Zulu nation was ready for war, and
that Natal was in danger of an invasion as great
as the Transvaal. Government officers, living on
the border, knew that war was inevitable."

But let us hear Ketchwayo himself at Cape
Town, in the account taken down from his lips by
Captain J. Ruscombe Poole, R.A., "who guar-
antees that every part of the story was fairly told

him by Cetywayo himself." After giving his story up to the time of his coronation by Mr. Shepstone, he says:—" Cetywayo saw he was losing his authority (when his soldiers pleaded sickness), so he sent out a regiment, and sent men down to the different kraals, and all absentees were slain, Cetywayo saying, 'You sick men are of no use to the country, so I will save the doctors the trouble of attending on you.' He also made an example of the women. He had ordered a regiment or class of women to marry the men of one of his regiments ; they complained to the King that there were too few men. The King gave in to them, and named another regiment ; but they made further objections, and a large number of them refused to marry. A regiment was called out, and sent to punish the refractory women ; and a large number were killed. Cetywayo said he 'was determined to show his people who was the master.' The young men in Zululand were getting very restless and quarrelsome, being anxious to get a chance of ' washing' their spears, *i.e.* bathing them in blood. *They were intent on having a war somewhere*, and proposed a raid into Swaziland solely for this pur-

pose (1877–78).　Mr. Shepstone told Cetywayo
that he must not go to war with the Amaswazi
(Swazis), as they were allies to the British.　Cetywayo, being pressed by his men, applied to the
English to agree to his making war with the
Swazis, and called up his army; but as the English
Government forbade it, he disbanded the army,
and sent them home.　The nation was very hostile
to the Boers on account of the frequent frontier
disturbances, and there is no doubt but that a very
little fuel to the fire already smouldering would
have brought on a war between the Boers and
Zulus.　Cetywayo himself was against a war,
although he threatened to fight the Boers; but
admits that, had not the Transvaal been annexed,
it was only a question of time how soon war would
have broken out between the Boers and Zulus.
The Zulus had no animosity against the English.
Cetywayo states that nothing would induce him to
disband his army.　John Dunn had used every
persuasion to prevent Cetywayo going to war with
the English."—See the whole story as given in
" Macmillan's Magazine " for February 1880.

The remedy for the present distress in Zululand

is to give the British Resident full power, and to appoint magistrates in every chieftain's district. In short, to give them thorough British rule through their own chiefs and our magistrates, as in Natal. I should also advise that the Governor of Zululand should have a personal acquaintance with the people, their language, manners, and customs, that he should reside in a central district, and should have a good large fort and a strong garrison; that he should avoid taxation, if possible, and not allow alienation of land on any pretence. Zululand for the Zulus.

THOMAS B. JENKINSON.

SIDMOUTH,
18th July, 1882.

CONTENTS.

AMAZULU.

PART I.

Description of Natal.—Manners and Customs.

I wish to review the past briefly, for the benefit of my friends at home and others who have never seen this part of the world, my object being to present a truthful picture of what I have seen and known myself. I do so in the hope that others, younger, stronger, and better than I am, may be induced to come and settle here as missionaries to the heathen or as good colonists.

I shall first endeavour to convey an impression of the appearance of the country and its climate, and describe briefly the vegetable productions, plants, trees, animals, and inhabitants as they have come under my notice.

1

Natal is a very hilly country—mountainous, indeed, on its western boundary, the Kahlamba or Drakensberg, rising to the height of 10,000 feet above the sea.

Recently I saw two very remarkable mountains, called the pillars (Insika), whence the name Ensikeni. The country there is called the forest country, from the fine forests which clothe the mountain sides. In times of war these forests become the places of refuge for the natives and their cattle. For example, there is now living in that neighbourhood an old man who, when a boy, fled for refuge from the Unkomanzi (near Springvale) to Ensikeni, about sixty miles, the Amazulu following, and killing men, women, and children. A few escaped in a fastness (inqaba) and came back. Soon after their return home, they were surrounded by cannibals from a remarkable hill in sight of Springvale Church, and again driven away.

The coast along the Indian Ocean is almost tropical, and produces the best sugar in large quantities, besides some coffee, tea, pine-apples, custard-apples, mangoes, bananas, oranges, lemons, and grapes.

Of course these are not indigenous, but are all

planted by the hand of the white man. The indigenous fruits are very poor, the most common being the Cape gooseberry and the amatungulu plum, which grows abundantly near the coast.

The coast district is naturally very thickly wooded, chiefly with low brushwood, though some of the trees are of fair size.

In places you might fancy yourself in an English park, with its clumps of trees and green glades.

Natal is also a well-watered country, although the years 1876 and 1877–8 were very dry, and most of the smaller streams were dried up. Some attribute this drought to the great destruction of the trees along the coast to make room for the sugar plantations. If this be the case, it is much to be lamented, for there is no doubt that these plantations have caused a rise in the price of maize, and have also introduced the use of rum of a very pernicious quality amongst the natives and low-class coolies and whites.

It is, however, a well-watered country, a land of brooks of water, of fountains and depths that spring out of valleys and hills.

The river valleys are in some places of enormous depth and extent, and clothed with trees and bush.

The valley of the river Unkomazi is remarkable
for the grandeur of its scenery.

The view from the top of a mountainous height
called Inkonya, about nine miles east of Springvale,
is certainly the grandest I have ever seen. You
look sheer down from the top of precipitous rocks
upon a wide-spreading and well-wooded valley of
great extent, and see the river winding like a
shining serpent far far beneath. Here and there,
dotted up and down, are the Kafir kraals, circular
huts, like hives, placed in a circle, with a well-
defined round cattle-kraal in the middle. The
height is so great that men and cattle can scarcely
be discerned below. All round from this hill the
view is magnificent, and the sea is discerned forty
miles off in the distance. The top of the splendid
hill is just like a gentleman's park at home. The
trees upon it are large enough for timber, but there
are but few of them. About the middle is a small
wood, and close by a pond formed by a spring of
delicious water issuing out of the rock. Hard by
is a precipitous descent into the valley. Here the
giant rocks seem to have parted asunder, wide
enough to admit of a very steep road or flight of
steps from top to bottom. The rocky walls are
about eighty feet high, and as perpendicular as a

castle wall. Just below the entrance a large tree has fallen across the chasm.

The whole gorge is a most remarkable one, and almost secluded and unused. It is cool and damp and shady on the hottest day.

Grasses.—The whole country is most verdant. Grass everywhere to the top of the highest hills; grass, too, of all sorts, from short sheep-turf up to the giant tambootie, like rye-straw, largely used for thatching.

Ferns.—Beautiful ferns abound.

The maiden-hair fringes the banks of the rivers.

The plants that remind one of home are the red clovers, buttercups, and peppermint, sorrel, and a few others, such as the iris, both yellow and white, and lobelia, both white and blue, and purple, which grows wild abundantly, and the geranium, which also grows wild. There are several plants like ours, and some briars; but not a single tree or bush or shrub growing wild have I come across that even resembled any of ours, except, perhaps, one that looks something like box at a short distance off. Jasmine grows wild abundantly.

Trees.—Mimosa thorns abound near Springvale and in the valley of the Unkomazi. These indicate a dry, warm climate. The river valleys are full of

trees of short stunted growth for the most part.
The most common are the mimosa, which makes
the best firewood, and whose bark is used for
tanning, and which yields a profusion of gum.
Aloes abound ; these lose their lower leaves, and
at a distance resemble the human figure. They
bear a splendid coral-coloured flower in the month
of June. One of unusual variety and size has
been planted in the garden at Springvale, and bears
a lovely pink flower of delicate hue and shape.

The country is quite bare of trees between the
Unkomanzi and the Umzimkulu. Beyond that
river is Griqualand, where forests clothe the
mountain sides, and where timber of good quality
is cut (*vide* p. 2).

Near Springvale there grows a wood resembling
red ivory, called umnini. Huge trees of cactus
and euphorbia abound in the valleys. As to planted
trees and fruits, there is scarcely one which we
have in England that will not and does not thrive
when planted.

In our garden we have apples, pears, peaches,
apricots, nectarines, mulberries, loquats, figs, and
custard-apples, besides oranges, lemons, medlars,
raspberries and strawberries. These keep up a fair
supply all the year round, which may well be

described as a perpetual summer compared with England. Winter there is none, except sometimes at night in the month of June—sharp hoar frosts.

Climate.—I can scarcely say, however, there is no winter. The winter is marked by intense drought, hoar frosts and cold winds at times, with a scorching sun. The grass becomes dried up and the smaller streams cease to flow and trees lose their leaves. Medical men would do well to observe that *colds* occur in the dry season, severe *influenza* in severe drought and not in the wet season, but this may be owing to the very sudden and violent changes in the temperature. It is anything but a temperate climate. Invalids would do well to avoid the months of May, June, July, August, and September here.

Insects.—Insect life is very abundant here. Butterflies are very plentiful all the year round. Some are very large and gaily coloured. Many of the white and blue and orange tips remind one of home, and the one called the painted lady is exactly like ours.

Locusts and ants are very common.

Termites, or white ants, are very destructive to buildings.

A winged ant swarms out of the ground about once a year, after rain, and after flitting about for a while, suddenly flings off its wings and creeps about. This strange creature is greedily devoured by all sorts of birds and poultry, and the little black children eat them as greedily as the fowls. Some large spiders weave almost silken webs— yellow. Birds are very common; swallows, partridges, quails, crows and rooks, and king-fishers remind one of England; but huge snake-birds, turkey bustards, panws, storks, vultures, besides numerous gaily-feathered ones, show a foreign country. Poultry do well without much care.

Snakes, Reptiles.—Serpents, snakes, adders, and vipers find this warm climate very congenial, though bites from them are very rare.

At times we are killing them almost every day, and sometimes two or three in one day.

Animals.—Wild animals are getting scarce here; but there are still leopards, panthers, and a few wild dogs, and the daman or *hyrax capensis*, called rock coney rabbit (a rhinoceros in miniature), and porcupines and antbears. Antelope and deer, too, are getting scarce.

Fifty years ago they abounded. There were

elephants, lions, and the lion's prey—the eland. Hunting is a favourite pastime with the natives ; they drive the deer, forming long lines. Cattle and sheep are numerous.

Herds of cattle form the chief wealth of the natives. They form part of the hereditary estate, and cannot be parted with readily. The calves are taken into their houses or huts at night, like children of the family.

Goats, too, are kept in large numbers.

On the high grounds the colonists thrive as sheep-farmers. Sheep sell now for £1 each. The sheep are small, like those of Wales and Yorkshire.

Horses are kept largely both by natives and white men. I lately met a chief in Griqualand attended by 200 mounted followers. Your ragged servant often has horses and cattle at home.

Husbandry.—Agriculture is in a rude state amongst the natives, who grow maize or Indian corn and millet or Kafir corn, sweet cane, the earliest green food, pumpkins, water-melons, underground beans, some sweet potatoes and herbs.

The women formerly did all the work with the hoe ; now ploughs and waggons are common all over Natal. Women and girls still do most of the hoeing and harvesting, which latter is a very easy process, as the weather is always dry and settled at harvest-time, *i.e.* May, June, and July. The corn is sown in September, October, and November, the wet and warm season, though in 1878 no rain fell till the end of October. Oats and barley grow fairly, and even wheat on the high grounds towards the mountains.

The present price of land is from 4s. to £2 an acre, but it is not readily obtained. When I left the colony Crown lands were being let at 1d. per acre for six months, in lots of 3,000 acres. In the Transvaal lands of 6,000 acres in extent could be bought at 6d., 9d., and 1s. an acre. Price in Natal from 4s. to £1 per acre in the country.

The natives plough a piece of land in the open plain or near the banks of streams, leave it un-enclosed, and sow the same ground year after year until it is worn out, then they abandon it for another piece. The only manuring the land receives is from the cattle who overrun it after harvest, and find much food in the amabele fields. They are the gleaners. As long as the country will bear this simple plan, the white man will not be able to compete with the natives in growing Indian corn. Live fences are fatal to corn crops,

and irrigation alone will enable the colonist to compete with the native ; but irrigation can only be carried out in a few places. It is largely practised at Doorne Vlakte, near Springvale on the river Ixopo, where a white farmer grows about 1,500 sacks of maize yearly, and supplies sugar-planters with 120 sacks of Indian meal monthly. He has a corn-mill on the river driven by water.

The question of the tenure of land is of such great importance that I here insert a brief description of the same as it exists in this part of the world. In their natural state the natives held their lands of the chief, and rendered him service, both civil and military, as in feudal tenure. Ownership of land amongst the people does not seem to have existed, only the temporary ownership of occupation. White men living under a native chief obtained the right of occupation, not ownership. So, when Bishop Callaway went to settle in Pondoland, he went direct to the chief, Umqikela, and got leave to settle near the Umzimvubu (St. John's). For this the chief would not expect any return in rent, and would probably get all he could out of the Bishop as his vassal. In Natal the natives occupy ten large native locations apart from the whites ; but now, the number having risen from 100,000 to

400,000, these locations are too small for them, so
they are found also squatting on Crown lands and
living on the farms of white men, as well as on
Church lands and in the towns. Under farmers,
natives usually are bound to furnish labour at
usual rates of wages. They are held in a state of
semi-serfdom, except that they are free to leave.
On all lands they pay a tax of 14s. a hut to the
Crown. This tax was raised from 7s. to 14s. on
the abolition of the £5 marriage tax in 1876.
On many lands they pay rent.

The Land and Colonization Company hold much
land and employ agents to collect rents. This last-
named tenure is most objectionable, and is the most
likely to cause disaffection. It does not seem fair
that a company should be allowed to occupy the
lands in this way. Government lays a non-occu-
pation tax on such lands.

People.—White colonists are few and far
between. Our nearest neighbour lives four miles
off. There is but one white man's house between
Springvale and the Umzimkulu, 30 miles by waggon
road. There is but one between us and the coast
district, 37 miles the nearest way. There is no
house between Springvale and the ferry over the
Umkomanzi river, 12 miles. But the Zulu-Kafir

natives swarm ; they swarm in the valleys, they swarm in the open country, they swarm everywhere. Their huts and kraals are often so hidden away that the country does not look thickly inhabited, but it is so, compared with that time when Captain Allen Gardiner, R.N., petitioned the Governor of the Cape to constitute it a British colony (1835), when, he says, " In consequence of the desolating wars of Chaka the whole country is unoccupied and uninhabited."

The natives are healthy, well formed, and well off. At present they are very well off, owing to their occupation of so much land. There are native locations all over Natal. A glance at Mair's large map will show how very much land is set apart for the natives as native locations, so that they may be kept distinct from the whites. Their frugality and simplicity of manners keep them healthy. Their food is maize porridge and pumpkins, milk, and beer.

I must now, however, go a little more into details about the natives, as our mission is to them, and to enter into the spirit of that it is necessary to understand something more of them.

Races.—Of the races not European now living in Natal, probably the greater number are Zulu-

Kafirs so called, but there is a great mixture of clans and races. There are still a few bushmen (abatwa), the wild men of South Africa. An account of one little bush girl has been published by the Society for the Promotion of Christian Knowledge. She was taught at Springvale and died in England. The Hottentots are found here but rarely. The Griquas are half-breeds, partly Dutch and partly Hottentot.

Indian coolies, chiefly from Madras, are largely employed in the cultivation of the sugar-cane. They take kindly to the country, and are settling down there in large numbers.

At Capetown there are Malays, formerly slaves, but now free ; they are the coachmen and cab-drivers, fishermen, and workmen of Capetown. They are a sober and industrious people, well dressed, and well-to-do. Their weekly holiday is Monday, when they go out into the country and amuse themselves with dancing in the groves. They are Mahometans. Dr. Arnold is our missionary to them.

The Boers are descendants of the old Dutch colonists, and many of them were French Hugue-nots who took refuge in Holland. They severed the tie which bound them to Holland when they

broke away from the restraints of the old Dutch
Government at Capetown and went into the wilds
to seek homes in the Free State and Natal.

Cannibals.—Not very long ago, _i.e._ within the
memory of man, there were cannibals even in sight
of Springvale and in other parts of the country.
A very good account of them (Amazimu) is given
by a native and published in the " Traditions,"
&c. " The Amazimu forsook their fellow-men and
went to live in the mountains. For at first they
were men like ourselves. The country lay desolate; there was a great famine—men were in want.
They began to seize other men and to devour
them, and so were called Amazimu (gluttonous).
With them men became game. They no longer
tilled the soil, no longer had cattle, houses, or
sheep. They lived in dens and caves, and hunted
men " (_vide_ p. 2).

The following is an account which (according
to Bishop Callaway) black men give of their origin
(it is translated from the Zulu) :—

" It is said the black men came out first from
the place whence all nations proceeded, but they
did not come out with many things, but only with
a few cattle and a little corn and spears and hoes,
and fire to cook their food, and potters' earth, and

wisdom which suffices to help ourselves when we
are hungry. We thought we were wise, and that
there was nothing which we did not know. But
now when white men have come with waggons,
that made us wonder exceedingly.

"We saw that we black men came out without
a single thing. We came out naked; we left
everything behind, because we came out first.

"But as for the white men, we saw that they
scraped out the last bit of wisdom. We came out
in a hurry; but they waited for all things.

"Therefore, we honour them, saying, ' It is they
who came out possessed of all things from the
Great Spirit—possessed of all goodness. We came
out possessed with the folly of utter ignorance.'

"We are now children 'in comparison with
them.

"As to their victory over us—they were vic-
torious by sitting still and not by armies. We
were overcome by their works, and say, 'These
men who can do such things, we ought not to
contend with them; if their works conquer us,
they would also conquer us by weapons.'

"The great wisdom of the white men over-
shadows all our little wisdom in which we used to
trust, which Unkulunkulu gave us."

Here I insert their account of the first missionary, also a translation.

" On the arrival of the English in this land of ours, the first who came was a missionary named Uyegana (Van der Kemp). He taught the people, but they did not understand what he said. He used to sleep in the open air.

" He went up the country and met with two men, a Dutchman and a Hottentot; they interpreted ; we began to understand his words. Two men of mark became believers; one remained at home, the other united with Uyegana. He, Unsikana, composed a hymn, called the Hymn of God. His faith was wonderful. To this day that hymn is a great treasure among the Amaxosa. Part of the hymn runs thus:—

Thou art the Great God, who art in heaven,
Thou Shield of Truth,
Thou art the Creator of Life,
Who madest the heavens, the Stars and the Pleiades.
Thou art the Leader—the Mantle which covers us.
Thou art He whose hands and feet are with wounds, whose
    blood was shed for us.
For this great price we call,
For Thine own place we call."

I wish now to speak of the language of the children of nature.

Language.—" The Zulu," says Bishop Callaway, " is a highly-elaborated language, much more so than the Hebrew, which in some respects it resembles.

" It is the language of a pastoral and agricultural people; of a people thinking gravely and cleverly within a certain circle of thought; of a people among whom exist rights of property and of citizenship in a certain sense; a people among whom peaceful pursuits were more acceptable than warfare; an intensely superstitious people, who, being unable to explain the phenomena of nature, referred them to spiritual agencies, which, however, they attempted to control by incantations and medicines."—Z. L. 1870.

The late Dr. Bleek, of Capetown, divided the South African languages into two great branches— the Hottentot or the Northern, and the Kafir or Southern. He remarks, truly enough, though curiously, that " among the Hottentots, as among northern nations, milking of cows is woman's work, whilst among the Kafirs a woman is not allowed to touch cattle or enter the cattle-kraal."

Dr. Bleek calls the Kafir dialects " Alliterative or Bantu." Two grammars of the language were published in 1859—one by the Bishop of Natal, the other by the Rev. Lewis Grout, American missionary.

Bishop Colenso says the Zulu-Kafir is the dialect of a small tribe which, under Chaka, acquired supremacy over the natives along the south-east coast of Africa. Natal is occupied by a very mixed population of Kafirs ; some of them are sprung form the aborigines, others have come in from all quarters.

Bishop Colenso has published also a dictionary and translations of the Bible, Prayer-book, the " Pilgrim's Progress," and other works.

Both Bishop Colenso and Bishop Callaway have made themselves masters of the language, although they did not begin the study of it until 1854, rather late in life.

A list of Bishop Callaway's works is given in my " Church Missions in Natal."

The following is a good example of the native language :—

" *Ba hambe ke, ba ye kuleyo 'nyanga e nukwe i leli 'buda.*"

" They go to the doctor whom the diviner has pointed out."

" *Ba ya ba fika ke kuleyo 'nyanga.*"

" They reach the doctor's."

" *Ba ngene endhini.*"

" They go into the house."

" *Ba ti, ' Sa ni bona.' "*

" They say ' We still see you.' ' We salute you.' "

" *Ba vume, be ti ' Yebo 'makosi.' "*

" They agree, saying ' Yes, sirs.' "

" *Ba ti, ni vela pi na ? "*

" Whence come ye?"

" *Ba ti si vela kwiti.*"

" We come from our own folk."

" *Ni hambela pi na ? "*

" Whither are you going?"

" *Si hambele kona lapa.*"

" We have come to this place."

" *Ini e ni i babele lapa na ? "*

" What business have you here?"

" *Ba ti, ' O, 'makosi si ze enyangeni yokwelapa. Si ya gulelwa.' "*

" O, sirs, we are come to the doctor who treats (of medicine).   We are sick at home."

" *Ba ti, 'Ikona ini po kwiti lapa na inyanga yokwe lapa?' "*

" They reply, ' Is there any doctor of medicine here ?' "

" *Ba ti, O 'makosi—si ye kuyona.*"

" We have come to him."

" *Ba hleka endhlini.*"

" Those in the house laugh."

After some more conversation like this the doctor is pointed out, and he says:

" What have you brought for me ? "

" *Ni ze nanto ni na ?* "

They say:

" *'Nkosi, ka si ze naluto.*"

" We have not come with anything."

" *Si zoku ku kipa, into i sekaya-imbuzi.*"

" We (will give you) to take you out of your house something which is at home—a goat."

He says:

" Is it possible that you come to take me away with a goat? "

They say:

" *O 'mgane, u nga zikatazi ngokukuluma, nenkomo i sekaya.*"

" O, dear sir, don't trouble yourself with talking, there is a bullock at home."

And so on.

The strong point of the language is that the verb by very slight changes is made to express so much, as the branches of the Hebrew verb *kal, paal, pihel, hiphil, hithpael,* e.g.,—

uku bona, to see.

uku bonela, to see for, look to.

„   *bonisa*, make to see.

„   *bonisisa*, to see very clearly.

„   *bonisana*, to help each other to see.

bonana, one another.

zibona, oneself.

zibonela, to look to oneself.

ziboneka, to become visible.

These simple changes—*ela, isa, ana, eka,*—may be rung on almost any verb, so regular are they. The passive is regular, and formed by *u, a,* or *wa* (as *bonwa*); and passives are used more frequently where we should use the active, as *ku fiswe,* "it is longed for," *i.e.* "they long"; *kwa fiwa,* "it was died"; *ku ya fiwa,* "it is time to die."

Another peculiarity of the alliterative dialects is that the noun projects a portion of its prefix upon every other word in the sentence that is related to it, as *umtwana wami omuhle u file*; here we have the letter *u* appearing three times.

Another peculiarity is the scarcity of adjectives except for colours and dimensions. Another is the very frequent use of the infinitive mood instead of the noun, especially for abstract ideas—as *ukulunga,* "to be straight" = righteousness ; *ukupila,* "to live," for "life." This verb is also used in other forms where we should use the noun—as *Opili-sayo abantu*, " He who gives life to man." " We owe life to ourselves alone," *Si zipilela nje.* And so John vi. 33 ought to be translated *opilisayo abantu* and not by the verb " give " and the noun " life."

On the whole we may say, that although European children and young people under twenty readily acquire the language if they mix with the natives, it is very difficult to acquire as you grow older, and a hard task indeed at forty. Language generally rules the religion and moulds our thoughts, keeping them in certain grooves. So many object to their children learning Kafir, and some think we ought to teach the natives English. This is easier said than done. A teacher from England ought, I think, to begin by trying to teach English, as this at once places him above his scholars, and he will thus learn their language by the way.

MANNERS AND CUSTOMS.

I now proceed to speak of the manners and customs of the natives, and of their religious system.

They used to practise circumcision universally, but Chaka put a stop to the practice among the Amazulu. Contact with the Arabs at some period may have been the means of introducing this. The Kafirs got their name from them. The Mahometans call infidels Kafirs. They have ceremonies for the coming of age both of boys and girls. They have sacrifices on such occasions to the shades of their ancestors—Amatongo. They believe in transmigration of souls. People turn into snakes at death.

They are polygamists, and the bridegroom pays a dowry of cattle to the father of the bride, as in old patriarchal times in Canaan and Ireland.

There are strong resemblances between the Kafirs of the present day and the ancient Irish living under Brehon Law and the Patriarchal System,* as is ably shown by D. Fitzgerald, Esq., *Fraser's Magazine.* The hereditary chief is in high repute amongst them. Almost divine honours were paid to him. Chaka claimed sovereignty above as well as on earth. His father was thought to have ascended on high. The great faith in

* Bishop Callaway notes the curious coincidence of thought between the Amazulu and Irish regarding the " good people."

Ulangalibalcle's powers as rain-maker was due to the fact that he, as a chief, had ability to contend with the heavens.*

Chiefs summon their wives to the royal hut, common men visit each house separately. If a chief's daughter be seduced, the offender must pay the whole dowry (as in Levitical Law), whether the father give her in marriage or not.

The Jewish law does not obtain amongst them in such cases. At the feast of first-fruits the people bring of their fruits to the chief before they taste themselves.

The people cultivate for the chief in the royal gardens. He is their father, they his children. He does not use his own hands for work, but allows his nails to grow like eagle's claws. In time of war he used to lead the army, though this practice was given up because his life was too precious to be risked. On a chief's accession he calls diviners to come and consecrate him. He uses divination himself. At his death he does not die alone. On his funeral pile is burnt an ox, and then some of

---

* Chaka ordered the rain doctors to be killed, because, in assuming power to control the weather, they were interfering with his royal prerogative. The doctors have medicines for treating the heavens.

his chief attendants. Sometimes in Zululand a great massacre celebrated the death of a royal personage. Whilst living, the name of the last enemy must not be breathed in his presence; after death his ashes were sprinkled on the water, and his spirit (*itongo*) entered into an imamba, or snake.

The chief is sole lord of the soil, and, as such, demands feudal service, both civil and military, of his vassals.

The only chief who is recognised as one in possession of land, having freehold tenure, is Umnini, whose place used to be the country down the coast below the Bluff at Port Natal.

Two sons of this man, educated at Zonnebloem, are at Springvale and High Flats. Their father paid me a visit. He told me that these days were no better than Chaka's.

The Bishop of Capetown, June 9th, 1850, says: "I have heard to-day that the Chief Umnini (of the Amatuli) removed from his lands on the Bluff last Friday. It was not without sorrow that he quitted his birthplace, where he withstood the troops of Chaka, who brought into subjection all the chiefs except Umnini and one other."

War, &c.—It is supposed that these people have

lived in a state of warfare with each other from time immemorial, being perpetually driven, and so, like the Arabs, have adopted a semi-nomadic life, and dwellings which could be forsaken at a moment's warning with but little loss.* The attack is usually made just before dawn. A male captive in war is made a slave or bearer of burdens to the captor, and often becomes a freed man and one of the family. (Deut. xx. 11.) Though not allowed to intermarry with his captor's children, he becomes his heir in case of the failure of his house.

The diviners are the appointed teachers of the people, a relic of an ancient priesthood.

They point out offenders, discover criminals (like our detectives), direct the sick to the doctor of medicines, trace the causes of sickness, find out the secret poisoners, witches, and wizards. They are duly initiated, and have to take their degrees. " He begins by being ill, which is caused by the Amatongo; he has many goats killed for him, and

---

* " This has been the fate of every African empire. A chief of ability arises, subdues his neighbours, and founds a kingdom. His successor cannot retain it, and in a few years the remembrance only of the empire remains. This normal state of African society gives rise to frequent and desolating wars."—Livingstone, " The Zambezi," ch. ix. p. 190.

he carries their gall-bladders in his hair." Once by
the road-side I came across a fine-looking woman,
almost copper-coloured, whose head-dress was a
mass of these bladders clustering up above her
head. She kept up an incessant talking, whilst a
young man sitting opposite to her kept exclaiming
" Izwa ! izwa! " (" Hear ! hear ! ").

Some divine by familiar spirits ; if not really
possessed, they must have the power of ven-
triloquism. But this would not account for their
extraordinary powers. The account given by the
late native Deacon Umpengula of the state of the
native mind on the subject of their ancestor
worship and degraded state, is very good. His
account, too, of James, a renegade Christian, who
became a diviner, is one of the most touching
of narratives. At Pengula's death, this James
made his appearance at Springvale, and professed
to point out the Umtakati who had caused the
death of the deacon. The victim was with diffi-
culty rescued from being stoned and beaten to
death.

The people quite believe in the power of their
doctors to lay spirits, hold converse with the
spiritual world—Amatongo—treat the heavens
against lightning, and to bring rain. They are the

medicine-men of South Africa. Some seem to possess power over snakes like the snake-charmers of India.

Ancestor-worship, shown in the form of sacrificing cattle and goats to the Amatongo to avert evil, appears to be the chief form of the religion of the Kafirs.

They have a superstitious dread of witchcraft and charms and secret poisoning, which is no doubt practised to a great extent, as they are great herbalists and skilled in the knowledge of poisonous plants.

In the Zulu pharmacopœia, as compiled by Dr. Callaway, the native names of 290 medicines and their uses are given. After copying out these my own remarks on them were as follows:—

They throw much light on the state of the people, a people subject to the ill that flesh is heir to, but especially to wounds inflicted in war by the poisoned spear and javelin, to snake-bites, sores, chest affections, coughs, colds and fevers, and diarrhœa. Reference is made to the spirit world, Amatongo, and to sorcerers and secret poisoners. Poisons are commonly named.

Great dread of death shows itself.

For physic, herbs are chiefly used, and the bark

of trees, with their leaves, twigs, and roots. Also parts of animals, birds, and reptiles.

Gross ignorance prevails, and a belief in charms, and war and love potions; great superstition, and an absence of all reference to a divine providence, and (as we should say) blasphemous pretensions on the part of the heaven doctors in treating the heavens for rain.

Here is no mere blank, but a system of divination, sorcery, and a slavish subjection to the doctors.

"Are there any of the vanities of the Gentiles that can cause rain."—Jer. xiv. 22.

They believe thoroughly in bad men and women who go about causing sickness and death. They believe that these abatakati go about at night, accompanied by familiars, wild cats and leopards and baboons, and lay poisons in the paths for people to step over, and on the thresholds, and in fields to destroy the crops.

Sickness and death are attributed to the malice and medical magic of these abatakati. Belief in these matters still clings to the natives after embracing Christianity. Among the outsiders it holds almost absolute sway, although they may be ashamed to own this to the white man.

Living on Springvale estate is a heathen man named Ungangati. One of his wives died, a diviner was consulted, and another wife was pointed out. She fled with her children to me. I sent for the man. He persisted in denying that she had been driven out. But she refused to go back, and went far away to her own people, children and all.

But this case dragged its slow length along for months.

Bishop Callaway has published an account of the religious system of the Amazulu, containing " The Tradition of Creation," " Ancestor Worship," " Divination," and there is to follow, the concluding part, " Medical Magic and Witchcraft."

This work, which followed his " Nursery Tales," is as valuable for its preservation of the *language* as spoken by the Amazulu, as it is for the *information* given concerning their state of mind and heart. Bishop Callaway's studies have led him to believe that the Zulus are a degenerated people, fallen from a higher state. He says, moreover, " We cannot reach any people without knowing their minds and mode of thought." What Sir George Grey felt was necessary for the government of the people of New Zealand the missionary will feel as necessary for himself, viz. a knowledge of their language and lore.*

The result of the researches of Bishop Callaway prove that these people have *traditions* of a *Creator*, but that he is "the unknown God" to them. "Unkulunkulu is no longer known."

The words of St. Paul to the Ephesians and Laodiceans are strictly applicable to them, "having no hope and *without God* (αθεοι) in the world."

Now a superstitious dread of disembodied *spirits* or of the *souls* of the departed entered into snakes —with sacrifices to such—a belief in divination and dealing with familiar *spirits*, and fears of witch-craft and poisoning ; these form the sum and substance of their religious system.

Certain practices, such as *circumcision, dowry of virgins, fines for seduction*, taking to wife a brother's widow, and feast of first-fruits, seem to indicate that at some remote period they had inter-course with the sons of Ishmael and Israel.

---

* " The African faith seems to be that there is one Maker of heaven and earth ; that sin consists in offences against their fellow men. Their idea of moral evil differs in no respect from ours. The only new addition to it (since the arrival of Europeans) is that it is wrong to have more wives than one. Men are connected with the spirits of the departed."—Livingstone.

Their present state, however, and past history seem to point to Ham as their progenitor.

This name *Ham* (warm and black in Heb.) is still a common name amongst them.

I have also met with the proper name *Toi*, the name of the King of Hamath the Great in North Syria; also a Hamitic name, to which also they do not attach any meaning that I am aware of.

Amongst their traditions preserved by Bishop Callaway is a distorted account of the dividing of the waters of the Red Sea for people to pass through.

The pretensions of the rain doctors and heaven doctors appear to us blasphemous. But they know not what they do.

" Africa is the oldest continent. The country looks as it did when it came from the hands of its Maker. The huts have no ruins ; the only durable monuments to be met with are mill-stones and *cairns*."—" Lake Zambesi."

They have a very curious custom of raising *heaps of stones*, each passer-by flinging his stone, with a prayer to the shades of their ancestors to grant them prosperity. Some think that this is a relic of the custom of raising a heap of stones over the dead, as was done over Achan and the King of Ai (Joshua vii.–viii.), and also over Absalom.

The law of inheritance in polygamic houses is
given by the late native deacon Umpengula in an
appendix to the nursery tales. Bishop Callaway
considers it identical with the law which prevailed
at the time of the patriarch Jacob. In other
respects they are behind the social status of the
patriarchs, besides being of an inferior race; rapid
improvement, therefore, is hardly to be looked for
from them.

A translation of Umpengula's summary of the
Zulu law on this subject is here appended:—

The Heritage in Polygamic Households.—The
account of the side of a polygamic house which is
called the side of the house of the boy who is the
little chief* of his father.

The women who are taken to wife by the cattle
of the eldest son's house,† become the heritage of

---

* The little chief of his father, that is, the heir-at-law,—
the next chief or head after the father. He is also called
inkosi, "chief." To avoid confusion I generally translate
such terms by heir, or eldest son.

† It is important for the understanding of this matter to
note the distinction made between the *kwabo-mkulu*, which I
have translated "the eldest son's house," and *kwabo impela*
(or, as expressed lower down, *kwabo-mfana*), which I have
translated "the eldest son's house in particular." The eldest
son born to the chief wife or *inkosikazi* has two inheritances
—the one hereditary, derived from his father, and father's
father backwards. This is the inheritance *kwabo-mkulu*, and
must descend from him, as it came to him by the law of

the eldest son; all of them are his heritage, together with those who are taken to wife by cattle of his house in particular, which are the offspring of a cow, which his mother gave him, which her father or grandfather gave her;* women taken to

---

inheritance, that is, of primogeniture. The other is derived from his mother—a cow or more given her by her father, or by a friend, or obtained by labour, becomes a new source of property, and is kept distinct in its appropriation from the paternal heritage. The difference is similar to that between entailed and personal property. But the entailed property of the native is invested in wives, girls, and cattle, and is necessarily as fluctuating as any other moveable property. The property of the eldest son's house (*ifa lakwabo-mkulu*) is the hereditary estate. Note, too, the expression *Abafazi bakwabo-leyo 'nkomo*, "The wives of the house of that cow."

* A new estate is commenced by gifts to the mother—by her labour—by girls whom she may have after giving one over to the chief house—or by gifts to the eldest son, or by his labour and by the labour of other children till they are married. If any such property is taken by the father to pay the dowry of a new wife, that wife belongs to the house to which the property belonged.

Some such custom, as regards marriage, as this here represented as in force among the natives must have existed among the people of Asia in the time of Jacob; and the account here given is calculated to throw much light on the history of his life and that of his children. By recalling that familiar history, and looking at it from a new point of view, we shall also be helped to understand better the state of the native law in such matters. It would appear that Leah was the inkosikazi or chief wife, and Rachel the second chief wife or hill. Rachel gives Jacob her maid Billah, that *she might have children by her*, that is, the house of Billah is a secondary house under Rachel, who is

wife by these cattle belong to the house whence that cow came, the son's house.* And even if the village at length become great through the wives of those cows,† the whole village is that boy's. If all the children of the several houses die, he is the heir of all their property; there is no one who can set up against him a claim, on the ground of its belonging to his side of the village, that is, on the ground that the women were taken to wife by cattle belonging to his house. They are not persons of another family; ‡ they are subject to him.

But as to a woman whom his father takes to wife by a cow which does not belong to the hereditary estate, but is his own personal property,

---

the chieftainess of the secondary great house, and the children born to Jacob in that house are Rachel's. Then Leah follows Rachel's example, and gives Jacob Zilpah, and Zilpah's house is a secondary house under Leah, who is the indhlu-nkulu or chief house. Reuben is the "little chief of his father," and Joseph the "iponsakubusa." His position, not only as the favourite of his father, but as the chief of the secondary great house, explains his dreams of superiority, and the jealousy of his half-brothers of the house of Leah.

* That is, the house of the eldest son—the house of which his mother is the chief.

† That is, the wives who have been paid for by those cows.

‡ *Lit.* They are not at a distance from him, but are so near to him that if the heir die, he becomes heir.

which is not regarded by the chief wife [as belonging to her], and which she cannot claim. [When
the husband comes home with such a cow,] he
says to the chief wife, " This cow, daughter of
So-and-so, is not a cow of your house, for I took
nothing from your house, nor from the hereditary
estate; it is my cow on which no one can have a
claim; I shall marry with it my wife, who will not
be a wife belonging to your house, but is my wife
only,—my village; for you are a wife whom I
took by my father's cattle."

The husband gains such a cow in this way,—
he cultivates a garden by himself, and the resulting
produce is not mixed with the produce of the chief
house, but is kept by itself, and he buys a cow
with it. Such, then, is the distinction between
that cow [and the cattle of the hereditary estate].
Or he may cultivate tobacco; he does not say the
tobacco-field is the chief wife's, but he says, "It is
my field," and he does not call the field by the
chief wife's house, for a chief wife can put in a
claim if a thing is called hers, when it has been
taken away again. The husband acts thus that no
claim may be made to such a thing.

When that cow, then, has increased, and he has
taken another wife by it, it is known that that wife

does not belong to the chief wife's house, nor to
the hereditary estate of the husband;* for nothing
has been derived from either for the purchase of
the cow. If the offspring of that cow are not all
taken for the dowry of the wife, those which
remain are the property of her house, and she is
called a hill.†

---

* The reader must bear in mind that in a large household
there may be distinguished the following houses which have
especial claims :—
  1. *Indhlu yakwabo-mkulu*, or *yakwabo-kandoda*. The hereditary estate.
  2. *Indhlu yakwabo-ndodana enkulu*. The house of the
chief wife. The eldest son is heir of the property derived
from both these. And the father cannot marry a wife by
cattle belonging to either of these without placing the new
wife under the chief wife, and whose house, *i.e.* heir, has a
claim upon the house of the secondary wife, which claim is
settled by the first-born female child becoming the property
of the chief house.
  3. *Indhlu yakwabo*, the house of a secondary or tertiary,
&c., wife.
  4. The husband has his private or personal property, with
which he can do as he pleases. This is the heritage of the
eldest son, if unappropriated at the father's death.
  5. *Indhlu yakwabo-ponsakubusa*. The secondary great
house (*indhlu-nkulu yobubili*), which is constituted by the
husband taking a secondary chief wife by his own private
property. This house has no right to inherit the property
of the great house but as the result of death carrying off
all the heirs of the great house. Neither can the heir of
the great house put in any claim to the heritage of this
house, so long as any male child belonging to it survives.
  † An *Intaba*, or hill, not a *ridge*. to which we give the
name of a hill, but a hill which stands out alone, without

Further, her son is called iponsakubusa,* that is, he is not chief; but in the village of his mother's house when it has become great he is the only head there, and is in no way interfered with.

When cattle remain after paying the dowry, the father may give his chief wife a cow that it may be the property of her house, if he does not wish that they should belong to the house of that chief wife which is a hill. If he wish, he can give the cattle to her, saying, " Here are the cattle of your house." She can make a claim on them if the husband marry a wife and does not place her under herself; she can make a great claim, saying, " Why is my village devoured?" She says

---

any connection with other hills. She is so called because she stands out alone—the commencement of a new house, owing nothing to the forefathers of the husband (*indhlu yakwabo-mkulu*), nor to the house of the chief wife.

* *Iponsa-'kubusa*, the-almost-a-chief. For he is not chief as regards his father's house; the eldest son of the chief wife is chief and heir of that, but he is chief and heir in the secondary great house. The place of the chief, in a kraal or in a hut, is on the right-hand side of the doorway. If the eldest son of the great house and the *iponsakubusa* are both at the same time in the hut, the eldest son sits near the doorway on the right—that is, the chief place—the *iponsakubusa* on the left of the doorway. But if neither the eldest son nor the father is there, the *iponsakubusa* sits in the chief place above all the other children, both of the great house and of his own. The *iponsakubusa* also sends the *insonyama* to the chief house.

thus because the husband says, " The wife I am
now about to take does not belong to your house;
she is my wife only." So that chief wife* starts
saying, " If you thus take your wife who has no
connection with me, what will become of my children's cattle ? Take of your own cattle, that what
you are doing may be right." The disputed right
arises in such circumstances as these.

Further, if the cattle with which the wife who is a
hill is taken are few, and the husband comes short,
and does not make up the requisite number with the
cattle which belong to himself, but takes some from
those of the chief house, the heir of the chief house
will put in a claim, and will not agree with the son
who is called the iponsakubusa, but will say, " No,
he too is a part of my house, for there are the cattle
of my house too among the cattle by which his
mother was taken to wife." If the father wishes
that that child which is the iponsakubusa should
not return to the great house, he may pay back
the cattle which he took by others, that the appointment of the father of that child may not be
futile and come to an end.

---

* That is, the chief wife of the other side—the hill. She
has the same right over cattle formally given to her by her
husband as the chief wife has.

And that child also has his side of the village, which has been derived from the cattle of that house ; and if there are no cattle of that house, if the father has cattle of his own, upon which no claim whatever can be made, he can enlarge that village by continually taking a wife, and declaring her to belong to that side, until it becomes a village ; all those wives are the heritage of that side.

If the iponsakubusa live, and the chief house come to an end, yet if there remain but one little boy of the last little house, the iponsakubusa cannot inherit the property of the chief house, whilst there still remains a son of the side belonging to the chief house. But if there does not survive even one boy, the iponsakubusa inherits the whole, and has no fear, but is a chief in every respect, since the real chief is dead.

Such, then, is the condition of polygamy. And such is the position of a husband in his house.

And the cattle of a man's father and his own cattle are distinct; the son says his father's cattle are his own when the father is dead ; but he too has his own which are distinct from those of his father, which his father gave him whilst living. For it is the custom for fathers continually to give cattle to their sons; not many, but one; but that one increases. When it has increased, the son may marry two wives at the same time; one he takes to wife by the cattle of his father, if he is still living; the other is the wife of his own cattle. There, then, are the two sides.

The children which are born from those two wives have not power throughout the whole village. The child of the father's cattle* claims superiority, saying, "I too in our village am a great man, for mother was not taken with the cattle of our common grandfather." But the son, whose mother was taken with the cattle of the hereditary estate, is the one that has authority in the village of the grandfather, if the grandfather has not another son who is chief; if the chief of the grandfather is the father of that son it is he who is head of the whole village.

But he whose mother was taken by the cattle of the father, does not remain in the village of the hereditary estate; he leaves, and has his own village by himself. And although he is inferior to him whose mother was taken by the cattle of the chief house, until he dies, yet then he takes

---

* That is, the *iponsakubusa*.

the chief place, if there is no one remaining belonging to the chief house.

If the chief house takes a wife with cattle belonging to it which comes next in order after itself; when that wife has a female child, she does not say the child belongs to her house; she knows it belongs to the chief house, and the cattle with which her dowry was paid is thus restored. And when she is married, the son of the chief house can take a wife with the cattle which have come as her dowry; and if he places her in the kraal as though she had been purchased by the cattle of the house of the girl by whose dowry she has been taken to wife, according to his own pleasure, he does not thus because he is afraid of a lawsuit, but because the village is his own. For example, Uzita married the mother of Ubabazeleni; she was the chief wife; she gave birth to Ubabazeleni, Uzita's chief son; after that cattle belonging to Ubabazeleni's house took to wife the mother of Unsukuzonke; Unsukuzonke was Ubabazeleni's brother, that if Ubabazeleni should die, and his offspring should die also, there might be no dispute among Uzita's children, but it be known that Unsukuzonke would enter on the inheritance, and would enter on it with reason, it being his property. After Unsukuzonke his mother had a girl; she grew up, and married Umathlanya. Uzita said, " The child is Ubabazeleni's." Unsukuzonke objected, saying, " Shall a child of our house be eaten by another whilst I am living, I who was born of the same mother as she?" Uzita therefore wondered very much at Unsukuzonke, and said to him, " If you try to eat the cattle of that child you will commit an offence, for your mother was taken to wife by the cattle of Ubabazeleni's house; this child belongs to his house; those that are born after belong to you." Unsukuzonke refused, and said, " Rather than that a child of our house should be eaten whilst I am alive, it is proper that I pay back those cattle, and I eat for myself." Uzita would not agree, but said, " If you take out* those cattle of your own accord, you will take yourself out of the chief-place; you shall no longer come next in order after Ubabazeleni; I will no longer know to what place you belong; † you shall be a mere man without a name in this

---

* That is, from your own herd, to pay back the dowry of your mother to Ubabazeleni. There is a play on the word *hipa*, " take out," which it appears best to preserve in the translation.

† That is, I will not acknowledge you as having any position amongst us.

village. You have now taken yourself out for ever.
I no longer know you for my part."

So Unsukuzonke refused, until at length he
ended by taking out the cattle; and so he was
taken out from holding the position second to
Ubabazeleni. And Unsilane was placed in the
position of Unsukuzonke, until Ubabazeleni's son
should grow up, and then he would give place to
him and return to the position of a brother, and
be the brother of the head of the house. But
when Ubabazeleni died, Umatongo, who was next
after Unsukuzonke, forgot that long ago his
brother took himself out of the headship, and
wished to enter on the government of the village;
but the men reminded him, saying, " You, Umatongo, have no longer any position here; there is
Unsilane, who will assume the headship of the
village." So he yielded.

So, then, all the children of a particular house,
which are born after the first girl, belong to that
house. The children from whose house a girl has
departed, will not follow her [to become the property of the great house]; the chief house is satisfied with that girl. But the children are still the
heritage of the chief house if all the heirs of that
house die. But if they are still living, the chief

house can touch nothing belonging to them; they
are under the chief house, because their mother
belongs to the polygamic establishment of the chief
house, because she was taken to wife by its cattle.
It is not said, since the cattle [with which the
mother was taken to wife] have now returned to
the chief house [by the first girl], they are no
longer under the chief house; they are under it
still, for if the chief house come to an end, it is
they who will enter upon the whole heritage. The
heritage is taken in the order of the houses as
regards the times of marriage. The heritage is
not allowed to pass by any house, so as to be given
to one who does not belong to the polygamic establishment of the chief house, until all are dead who
follow the chief house in order; at last the last
male child which belongs to the great house enters
on it. When all are dead who can properly enter
on the heritage, it is taken by those who are of
kin;* the heritage is taken by the house which
used to participate† with the great house when

---

* *Umdeni,* those who are of kin—those belonging to the
polygamic establishment of the great house, in the order in
which the several wives have been taken in marriage.

† All the houses under any particular house, whether the
great house, or the secondary great house, participate in the
meat of all cattle slain by any one house.

cattle were slaughtered. Such, then, is the mode
of inheriting. The heritage falls to all the houses
in order of their inheritances.* If all are dead to
whom the inheritance belongs, the iponsakubusa
takes it, for he takes it with good reason—it is now
his; no one will call him in question, for the whole
house has come to an end; and he takes possession
with reason, because his father and the father of
those of the chief house were one; he is not far
removed from his father's estate; when the chief
house comes to an end, the whole belongs to him.

Further, as regards the ejection of the first wife
from the chief place, she is ejected for two reasons
for which it is proper that she should be ejected.
She is ejected for adultery; if she has been guilty
of adultery before she has had a child, it is said
that it is not proper that her house should stand
at the head of the village. If she has had a boy,
she is removed from the house at the head of the
village, to the gate, or to the side of the kraal;
and another wife is sought who is a virgin, and not
one of those who were under her who has been

---

* That is, if the chief house fails of heirs, the heritage
falls to the second house; if that too fails, it falls to the
third, and so on. If all the heirs of the great house fail,
the next heir is the iponsakubusa.

ejected; and so she who is a virgin is taken to wife; and she who has been guilty of adultery is told, " Since you have destroyed your great name, the daughter of So-and-so will be taken to wife and fill your place, and become the mother of So-and-so," that is, the heir, the son who is separated from the mother on account of her offence, and placed with the new wife. If, then, she fills well that office, it is she who is the chief wife indeed; it is she who is the mother of the youth who has been taken away from his mother. And the children of the new wife are not chief; they come in order after the young chief who has been introduced into her house; the first child of this wife comes next in order after the young chief; and the property of his house is taken from his mother's house, and is taken to the chief house; it follows the boy to the place where he goes; there is left behind in the old house* only such little things as are necessary for his nother's existence.

So they settle down as regards that matter, it being now known that she was ejected for ever, and that the new wife is established as chief. If

---

* The old house—the house of the displaced chief wife.

she is a good woman and treats the boy with the greatest care, he forgets his real mother, and habitually goes to the new mother, no longer using himself to the real mother, but now using himself to the house of the new chief wife.

And she is ejected if she does not know strangers: for among black men the head house is that to which strangers from all parts go, and are treated well there; for the treatment of strangers is an obligation resting on the chief wife of the village. When we say to treat them, we mean to give them food, and to give it without weariness; not to know them is that she should grudge them food, denying that she has any, and, if there is any, concealing it, and eating it secretly unknown to them; scolding them, and turning them out of her house in anger. Among us such a wife goes out; she is not fit to *bear* the village; it is proper that she go lower and take her position at the entrance; and another take her place, who is able to fill it aright. Such, then, is the ejection of a wife from the chief place. Such, then, is her expulsion.

In daily life these people are singularly frugal and simple in their habits.

The men go naked except a kilt back and front.

They have no clothing, and know of none. In parts of Pondoland and elsewhere they go even without the kilt.

Even the head is always bare, and even shaven all exposed to the sun.

Sometimes the hair is allowed to grow, and is worked up into shapes like mitres, cones, or horns to the height of six or nine inches.

The men, on attaining a certain rank, wear the head-ring, which is made of the leaves of a plant carefully bound and bent into a ring and sewn to the hair. It is kept polished, and in shape reminds one of the old forage caps ; though in Griqualand, among the Amabaca, it is as small as a curtain-ring, and is seen perched up on the top of a cone of stiff hair. It is a sign of manhood and subjection to the chief.

The women wear a topknot of red clay, but often their hair hangs round their heads, covering their foreheads like a red mop.

The dress of the women is a rude skin petti-coat, the upper part of the body being quite naked.

The custom of smearing the body with red clay and grease prevails.

Both sexes are very fond of ornaments, necklaces, bracelets, armlets, and anklets, and feathers stuck in their hair. Charms of teeth and claws are much worn. In full dress the men always carry shields of ox-hide and weapons. Their weapons are spears and javelins, and knob-sticks ; they have no bows and arrows, though the bushmen have.

In agriculture the hoe is almost their only implement.

They make rude pottery, and weave mats and baskets of excellent quality.

They produce fire by friction, whirling one stick into another.

It is almost needless to say that they can be quite independent of the white man and his wares. To put this their primitive state in the negative form, we might say, they have no shops such as we have, no markets, no soap, coal, salt, or matches, no candles, no clothing, no hats or shoes, no drugs, no tea, coffee, sugar, bread or butter, no fruits except wild ones, and rarely any meat.

We think we live simply, but when we come to live amongst them we find our artificial wants and luxuries are great and many. We should think ourselves badly off without such things. They are very well off without them, and have much less sickness than we have.

Their dwellings are round wattled huts, thatched all over, like bee-hives. They creep into these, the man going to the right and woman to the left. The hearth is in the middle, and the smoke goes out through the door and thatch.

In a large kraal there are eight or ten of the huts, and in the middle of them is the almost sacred enclosure of the cattle kraal, where the cattle are penned at night, and where sacrifices and feasts of flesh meat take place. Underneath the cattle kraal are pits for storing grain, with a small secret aperture covered with a stone.

There are also wattled huts for the Indian corn and pumpkins, and sometimes a threshing floor for the millet amabele, fenced in neatly with thorns, and containing piles of Kafir corn for beer, whilst on the ground may be seen at times underground beans drying in the sunshine. The women grind the corn, as in the East, between two stones, kneeling at their work. They make porridge twice a day usually; though when Kafir beer is made, this serves for meat and drink. It is like sour gruel, very thick. Their principal food besides is *amasi*,* curded milk, and pumpkins,

* Strangers refuse Amasi coming from another kraal.

beans,* with a few vegetables, and honey. Flesh meat they seldom get ; when they do, they and their friends will finish an ox at a sitting.

They are much given to snuff-taking at all times, and grow tobacco for the purpose.

Some indulge in smoking wild hemp in a cow's horn.

In times of famine they take to roots and bulbs.

---

* Beans—both kidney beans and underground beans.

PART II.

PERSONAL NARRATIVE.

I SAILED from Southampton on the 5th March 1873, with my wife and three children. We reached Madeira in one week, and crossed the line the week following. On Lady-day we touched at St. Helena ; the island is bold and rocky, of volcanic formation, the rocks being reddish and purple. The inhabitants, besides the whites, are a mixed race of blacks, speaking English. The British exchanged Java for this island with the Dutch. American whalers touch here, though many ships now go through the Suez Canal, and so the St. Helena people go to the Cape and Natal for service. On the 2nd April we came to anchor, or in dock, at Capetown, where we were kindly met by Mrs. Espin and taken to the Kafir College, Zonnebloen,

where we stayed four days. Mr. Espin took me to
see the Diocesan College under Canon Ogilvie.
Preached at Papendorp twice for Espin. On the
9th we sailed for Natal, touched at Mossel Bay and
Port Elizabeth and East London, and reached Port
Natal on the 19th of April, just six weeks after
leaving England. I took Archdeacon Robinson's
duty at Durban for two Sundays, and then went on
to Maritzburg and Springvale.

Dr. Callaway kindly entertained us for some
time, until we took possession of his old house,
which we occupied during his absence in England.
There were two native deacons at Springvale, and
Mr. Broadbent, a Catechist, besides a teacher for
the girls' school. I taught the first class in the
boys' school during the bishop's sojourn in England,
whence he returned in October 1874. Umpengula,
native deacon, died in January 1874, and Heber,
suspected of causing his death, was assaulted and
stoned. For three months after these sad events a
deep gloom settled upon Springvale, and unusual
mortality prevailed the year following. Miss
Hayward arrived on the 10th February 1874, and
Humfrey Davis in March.

In May I paid my first visit to Clydesdale, the
place I had selected as the most suitable for myself

on being accepted by the S. P. G. My duties
during Bishop Callaway's absence consisted
chiefly in taking all the English services daily, and
on Sundays at Springvale; going over to Highflats for duty every fourth Sunday; teaching in the
day school in the morning, and copying out Zulu
manuscripts for reading the New Testament lessons
in church, and reducing to alphabetical order
a dictionary-appendix (Zulu). I also had the
management of the parish, and had to teach my
only son daily.

On the 28th June 1875, Bishop Callaway took
his departure for Kaffraria, and the next day the
remaining deacon and catechist left also—for good,
and I was left alone. Eight days after I preached
for the first time in the native language. Soon
after this I paid my first visit to the Umzinto,
Canon Barker being ill, and rode with my son
along the coast to Durban and Maritzburg, and
home. At the end of March the Bishop of St.
John's returned to Springvale.

2nd April, Charles Johnson agreed to come as
schoolmaster, and the Bishop took his final
departure three days after.

At this time Sir Garnet Wolseley arrived as
administrator (*vice* Sir B. Pine).

We have to thank him for the abolition of the
£5 marriage-tax on the natives.

H. Davis was ordained on Trinity Sunday.

I now succeeded Bishop Callaway as Chief Missionary of Springvale, and was installed as Canon
of Maritzburg, preaching at night in the cathedral.

Miss Hayward was very ill at this time.

In August, James G. Chater arrived to fill the
post of schoolmaster, Johnson going to Highflats.

In October, Broadbent arrived from Ensikeni,
and we gave him an offertory of £3 10s. for his
church.

In November I visited the Ixopo with the
Bishop of Maritzburg, where a meeting was held
and committee for building a school appointed.
On Advent Sunday bishop confirmed at Springvale
and baptised thirty natives.

This year we bought church plate for Highflats
with money raised at Highflats and Springvale.

1876.—In January this year I went to the pro-
vincial synod at Capetown, as delegate, and on the
7th March returned to Springvale, bringing with
me two sons of *Umnini*,* educated at Zonnebloen.

* "Umnini is the only chief in Natal who survived Chaka's
conquest, and is in possession of freehold land."

Again I was hospitably entertained at the college by Mr. Peters.

During my visit I paid a visit to an inland town, Stellenbosch, a quaint old Dutch town, with fine old tree avenues, some 200 years old. Here is a ladies' college and a boys' school or college—a Dutch *academe*.

April 1st.—The Marriage Tax abolished this day.

5th.—Canon Moore died.

For six weeks after my return I was unwell.

June 7th.—The Bishop of St. John's arrived and made over to me the Springvale Church Building Fund—£244.

On Trinity Sunday, in company with Bishop Callaway, I visited Richmond and Byrne, when the Bishop preached to natives in Zulu.

June 13th.—Henry Callaway, D.D., M.D., Bishop of St. John's, made over his property (3,000 acres) at Springvale and Highflats to the church, and my rent ceased.

August 10th.—Rev. W. Baugh died at Richmond.

Began to form a library for Springvale.

I published a statement called " Church Missions in Natal," a report with a review of the history of missions in that colony.

The village regulations passed, consisting of a preamble and ten heads of rules concerning 1, tenure ; 2, the council; 3, feasts ; 4, money matters ; 5, trespass ; 6, cattle ; 7, trees ; 8, grass burning; 9, river conservance ; 10, duties of bailiff.

1877.—This year opened with intense heat and great drought, the river becoming stagnant.

January 24*th.*—Engaged natives as quarrymen, and began to lay in a stock of timber for building the church.

On 26th February, after a fortnight's illness, died, Augusta Caroline Hayward, teacher of the girls, and organist—deeply lamented.

In April, the teacher of the boys, J. G. Chater, began to complain of illness, and went to Maritzburg to consult the doctor, who told him he must leave South Africa.

This month the Bishop of Maritzburg returned from England, and Miss Fox, from Warminster, arrived at Springvale.

In June and July I went several times to Richmond and Byrne, *vice* Archdeacon Fearne, disabled.

It was in July, too, that I began to feel disheartened and discouraged in my work.

About the same time Bishop Callaway finished printing his translation of the Gospel according to the Four Evangelists, printed at Highflats by J. A. Blair.

In September, Chater was again absent in Pietermaritzburg. Most intense heat prevailed, and one day five snakes were killed by my son during the dinner hour; one shot in a tree. Thermometer 100° in tent ; sun like fire. I was attacked with *ophthalmia* for the second time. The first time *I was blind for twelve days*; this time not at all blind, but quite unable to bear looking even at pictures for a moment.

Synod was held 30th October, when I read my report as Secretary for Missions.

Part of this was published in the " Mission Field " for April 1878.

October 15th.—Began to build the church.

21st.—Broadbent and William the deacon favoured us ; one preached morning, the other afternoon.

The next day Broadbent's horse and my saddle were stolen, but I recovered both in Richmond, riding seven hours in the rain. The thief tried to steal another horse, but was overtaken by the owner, who thus recovered both.

In November I paid a visit of some days to the Ixopo, and got the magistrate to appoint us a native village constable ; visited the white people, and held service on the Sunday.

In December Mrs. Jenkinson became very ill indeed.

1878.—At the beginning of this year I became very unwell and downcast.

A curious phenomenon occurred 7th January. A bright star appeared near the moon at noonday, the sun shining brightly. *Omen.*—The natives from this foretold the coming war with the Amazulu. Intense heat and drought prevailed at this time.

January the 25th was the hottest ; thermometer 105° on E. side under thatch on the verandah from 12 noon till 4 P.M., when it fell two degrees only.

February 3rd.—My diary says : " The daily congregations have never been so good as now since I came, making allowance for the sixty people who have left. I should say that the congregation has largely increased, especially by young men and outsiders." They come to pray for *rain* chiefly.

March 2nd.—Bishop Callaway arrived in his carriage drawn by two horses and six mules, and preached on the Sunday, besides conversing in the most cordial manner with the natives on Sunday and Monday, when I accompanied him to High-flats. Here we were detained two days by the *rain*. My horse falling sick, the bishop kindly took me up into his carriage, and we drove on to Clydesdale, where we were kindly entertained by Mr. Button; F. A. Broadbent, of Ensikeni, was also there.

On the Saturday I attended a large meeting of chiefs and headmen, who were addressed by D. Strachan, the magistrate, who speaks the language better than any one Englishman. An outrage had been committed at Kokstad, and the Griquas were known to be disaffected. Strachan's aim was to conciliate Usidoi, chief of the Inhlan-gwini, who, however, did not attend the meeting. Usidoi was an outlaw from Natal. Next day, at Bishop Callaway's request, I preached the Ordination Sermon on the occasion of the ordina-tion of Mr. Tonkin. The school chapel was quite full, and the Bishop addressed the Griquas by an interpreter in *Dutch*.

Next day the Bishop, accompanied by myself and Mr. Broadbent, went on to Ensikeni, about eight hours' journey on horseback, to the north-west.

We met Usidoi, the chief, coming to see the magistrate. The Bishop halted at a kraal where a white man kept a store in a Kafir hut. Breakfast was set out on a low box, with a newspaper for a table-cloth, and other boxes for seats, the accommodation, however, *being unusually good.* The Bishop said, " I knew we should have a good breakfast, Mr. Smith, when I heard it was you."

The carriage could proceed no further. The mystery was how it could have come so far without breaking. One hill was almost precipitous and too steep both up and down for anyone on horseback even. We all proceeded on horseback through a splendid country; the prominent mountain peaks of the Insika,* 6,000 feet, being clearly visible all the way. On arriving at Ensikeni, I was greatly surprised with the beauty of the mountain and forest scenery, but felt so much the loneliness of the place for Broadbent, that I spoke to the Bishop about it. I found no less than thirty-eight old Springvale people here, about seven of whom were confirmed together with six Basutos and others.

---

* Insika—Zulu for " pillars " ; peaks bearing up, as it were, the canopy of heaven.

Broadbent accompanied us back to the half-way kraal, and then we parted—alas! never to meet again in this world, I fear, as we were wont to do.

Two things struck me very much in Bishop Callaway's treatment· of the natives throughout this visit—the ease with which he conversed with them, and his deep compassion for their state; and yet when speaking to the candidates he used notes and manuscript.

War broke out. Broadbent was reading for his priest's ordination. He became anxious for his people and his place; lost sleep and appetite; and then, after making arrangements for their safety, he quite broke down.

Poor fellow! On Easter Eve (I cannot write without emotion), after twelve hours' waggon-journey, night and day, accompanied by Humfrey Davis, he was carried into Springvale rectory by myself and others, and caused us the greatest alarm and anxiety until Monday, when Davis again took him by waggon into hospital at Pietermaritz-burg.

To me this is the most painful event I have ever had to record. Poor Broadbent was our friend and brother for nearly two years at Springvale, and his new mission in Griqualand among the Amabaca, Griquas, and Basuto people of three different tongues, was the most promising I have ever seen.

Broadbent had been engaged incessantly in mission-work for eight years, and was ordained deacon by the Bishops of St. John's two or three years since.

He was quite an enthusiast and true evangelist (rare qualities), thoroughly unselfish and self-denying.

A little before he broke down, J. G. Chater left Springvale on account of his failing health, and entered the new diocese instead of returning to England. He has been taking duty at Ensikeni since Mr. Broadbent left.

Peace was soon restored in Griqualand. Captain Blythe, D. Strachan, and Stafford attacked the rebels in their stronghold, utterly routed them, killing Smit Pommer, the Hottentot ringleader, and taking many prisoners, and returned to Kokstad in triumph. A terrible fate awaited poor Stafford and seven others. The powder magazine exploded and killed them.

Mr. Stafford was clerk to the magistrate, and had been successful in preventing Usidoi from joining the rebels.

I met this Usidoi with a following of 150 well-dressed mounted men on my way to Ensikeni. My friend. Broadbent reined up and conversed with him in a friendly way for some time. Most of the men recognised Broadbent, and greeted him.

April 25th.—The Bishop of Maritzburg arrived in his carriage, and I accompanied him to Highflats, where we found the school in good order under the Rev. H. Davis, assisted by Louiska Umnini of Zonnebloen, and one of my old scholars as pupil teacher. Mr. Blair, too, had been rendering good service, and Miss Beck, recently arrived from England. There were twenty natives confirmed.

After returning to Springvale we had seven guests to stay the night, and as many horses in the stable; and the next day I accompanied the Bishop on his visit to St. Elmo, a little school founded by Dr. Sutherland, some seven miles off. A native wedding feast was going on at Springvale, and the Bishop met the wedding procession. On this occasion the ox chosen for the feast, being rather wild, was shot by my son.

On the 5th of May the Bishop held a confirmation at Springvale, when eleven natives were confirmed and partook of the Holy Communion. The Bishop addressed the candidates through Mr. Johnson as interpreter. This Mr. Johnson, who began mission work under me at Springvale and Highflats, had carried on a very successful work at St. Faith's, Durban, for the past year; but being unable to stand the climate of Durban, he has resigned and has just gone towards the mountains north-west beyond Estcourt, to undertake the mission of St. Augustine's to the Basutos under the chief Hlubi. His place at Durban has been taken by Mr. Blair of Springvale.

Our land lies far away from the main road, and is flanked on the east by a large native location of 8,000 acres, a district of about six miles long and three or four miles wide in the broadest part; it is, therefore, a most favourable situation for a mission to the natives, who, on the whole, are very friendly and well behaved, though fast tied and bound with the chain of their own superstitious and social condition. They often dispute with each other in a way most wearisome to me, but furnishing apparently mental exercise to themselves.

Take, for example, a case which occurred last week:—

On Friday (14th June) Corry came to me in the vestry after morning prayers at 7.30, and stated that the man who had bought his horse for £10 had paid only £5 5s., and for the rest was offering lung-sick cattle.

" He that is first in his own cause seemeth just," &c., "but his neighbour cometh and searcheth him."—Prov. xviii. 17.

Presently the man Joannes, of Highflats, came in, and his friend, and then it came out that these two men had arrived the night before and that Corry had forcibly seized the horse.

I told him to restore it and try to agree about another ox, and as he would not listen to reason I wrote out a statement in duplicate and gave each a copy to take to the magistrate.

But lo! in the afternoon my man comes back humbled and convinced, gives Joannes his horse, and accepts the ox.

Take another case which happened this week at an outside kraal (at which, however, we have seven Christians, all baptised within the last three years).

On Tuesday, the 18th of June, I was told that Ungangati, Tambuza, and Utshingwayo, three heads of kraals, all polygamists, wearing the head-ring (the token of subjection to the chief), wished to see me. I went to them, and they told me in their own tongue, with much gesture and action (they speak while squatting), that Utshingwayo's two huts were burnt down the night before, with all his corn and clothing. I told them I was very sorry and would come and see the place. I went the next morning. The village constable being at the early service I summoned him to accompany me, and he was all ready with his horse saddled by the time I returned from my walk with my two little girls. We rode to the spot and found the embers and thatch still smouldering. It appeared that about ten o'clock the night before, Utshingwayo had retired to rest with his chief wife and several children, and four goats in the hut (the natives take calves and kids inside their huts at night), when suddenly the hut burst out into a flame, being set on fire from without. On rushing out, he saw his second wife just entering her separate hut. He had but just time to rescue his family and live stock before his own hut was burnt with all his goods, sleeping-mats, blankets, and clothing. Then the fire spread to the next hut, which was the wattled barn for his new crop of Indian corn ; thence to another and the second wife's hut and her store of corn. Next morning heaps of ashes and earthenware jars and pots burnt red with the fire, with half-burnt cobs of maize, were all that was to be seen of the little kraal. These were all heathen people; and the second wife, who ran away the next morning, is the suspected culprit. It was wonderful to see the calm, philosophical, and sensible view that the man took of his sad case. On this circumstantial evidence the whole of the people condemned the woman, and in their native state would probably have knocked her on the head without mercy.

20th.—This morning the man has gone in search of his runaway wife and to the store for blankets.

As to the general condition of the mission, although I am not in a mood to take a very hopeful view of things just now, I cannot fail to see progress, and that not here only, but in other parts of the colony and in the new diocese.

Mrs. Jenkinson has been very successful in her surgical and medical practice, which she can describe better than I can, also in teaching married women, in which she is very ably assisted by Miss Fox, who takes very kindly to the work, and is, so far, happy and well.

She has lately held a small night-school. My daughter's school of girls and little children has been very successful.

We have now three who can play the harmonium in church and school—my wife and daughter and Miss Fox.

All our Christians wear clothing, both men, women, and children. The suggestion made by the Dean of Manchester at the Oxford Congress, about dress, is impracticable chiefly because *we* do not dress them, except partially, through the Ladies' Association. They ought to be informed, perhaps, that the best dress both for men and boys is the *striped blue tunic skirt* with short sleeves, in two or three sizes. This makes a complete and becoming dress, if of good cut and made to reach to the knees. But the Dean's kind suggestion is also impracticable, because it is the storekeepers who furnish the clothing, and they take the cheapest they can procure at home, just what happens to be going at the time. Of course a blanket is the simplest and best, only they often leave them at home and go naked.

All our Christians give up polygamy of course. They live in fair cottages, which they make themselves of wattles. They come to church daily very regularly, but are seldom in time.

As I am now hoping to welcome another fellow-worker out from home very soon, nine months having elapsed since I wrote, I will say that *sound men* ought to be sent—men of good temper and common sense, not excitable or timid, not dependent upon society or amusement (of which we have little); men of great patience and perseverance, both in acquiring the language and in dealing with the natives. The one great principle which ought to rule a missionary's conduct and conversation, and which ought never to be lost sight of or abandoned, either in theory or in practice, is this, " Be not overcome of evil, but overcome evil with good." And this I take to be the very essence of the Gospel which brings "Glory to God in the highest, peace on earth, and goodwill towards men."

The field for missionary enterprise is almost boundless here, but the discouragements are very great, and these arise chiefly from our own countrymen.

Men coming out, then, should be forewarned. After hearing of so much sickness amongst the clergy (there have been four wardens at Bishop's College since I have been here, and three men at Durban), I need not say that some find the heat very trying at times.

It is very important that men should be able to turn their hands to anything, and yet they should

not do more in this way than is good for their
daily exercise or recreation; they should not lower
themselves in the eyes of the natives. It is well
that young men should take an interest in farming
and gardening, and in some branch of natural
history.

What we really want in this country is good
practical Christians, who will be jealous for God's
holy law, and not lower its standard whilst
they hold forth the word of life, the glorious
Gospel of the blessed God—men who will neither
spoil these children of nature, nor rule them
harshly; men who will have the courage to sacrifice the individual for the good of the community,
and to cut off the mortifying member to keep the
body sound.

Before leaving England a missionary ought to
resolve to give up all for Christ's sake, and be
willing to lay down his life for the brethren,
and then, after that, he need not fear. " Love
casteth out fear."

> Give me the priest these graces shall possess—
> Of an ambassador the just address,
> A father's tenderness, a shepherd's care,
> A leader's courage, which the cross can bear,
> A ruler's awe, a watchman's wakeful eye,
> A pilot's skill, the helm in storms to ply,

A fisher's patience and a labourer's toil,
A guide's dexterity to disembroil,
A prophet's inspiration from above,
A teacher's knowledge and a Saviour's love.

Bp. Ken.

Much is required in a thorough missionary. One other matter is that we must take good heed to hold our own. *Quod tuum tene*, κρατει ὁ εχεις, " Be not overcome of evil," for " Evil communications corrupt." " Φθειρουσιν ηθη."

One of the most sensible remarks on this subject was made by a Swiss missionary, Ernest Creux, in the Transvaal. He says, " How blind they are who will not allow the Kafirs to be educated. They do not see that, if they do not educate the blacks, the blacks will educate them. Do they not teach our children all their vice, their cunning and superstitions, and their impure customs? No one at home would believe how much their countrymen suffer here by associating with the natives. I will merely mention cases which have come under my own observation. Beginning with those early settlers who were corrupted by intercourse with the heathen, down to the latest comer from the mother country, all seem to suffer more or less from contact with heathenism, exemplifying the wisdom of that saying of Menander, as quoted by

St. Paul, and read in our ears at every burial service —'Evil communications corrupt good manners,' 'φθειρουσιν ηθη χρησθομιλιαι κακαι,' Many white men take heathen wives. One man, the brother and son of a Wesleyan missionary, a white man, deserted his wife and children, and ran away with a native girl ; two white men, of good education and connexion, ran away with two native Christian girls, promising them marriage, and then after a month or two cast them off; one white lady ran away with a black man.

But besides these notorious cases, it is very painful to find the white people generally suffering, often unconsciously, from loss of the society of their fellow-countrymen, and constant intercourse with the natives. White children frequently speak the Zulu-Kafir before they speak English. Even my own children used to hold their play-prattle in the native tongue, until I took away their black nurse, and put a stop to their going to the natives' houses.

Even the missionaries do not always escape this danger. No wonder, then, that young colonists, disappointed with the country, and deprived of home influence and comforts, yield to the enervating effect of the climate and to the temptations which beset their path."

The "Natal Government Gazette," 25th June, 1878, gives the code of native law as at present administered.

This law hinges upon a few leading principles, **viz.** the subjection of the female sex to the male, and the children to their father; primogeniture; the incapacity of women; polygamy, and adoption.

There are sixty-four clauses. No. 25 runs as follows. "The following diagram represents a kraal, and the position in it of the great wife and the rest:—

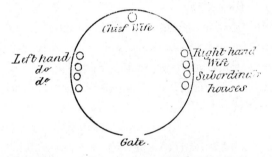

On the 13th of December 1878, the Zulu award and ultimatum was published, to be agreed to within thirty days. All that we can do is to hope and pray that it may please the Ruler of Princes to move the heart of the Zulu tyrant to agree to the terms proposed, and so avert a most terrible war. Our soldiers and volunteers are all on the border ready to invade the Zulu country. If they do, I

fear the slaughter will be most terrible. Men of
good family and position in the colony have left
their homes and professions to go to the front.
The Dean sends one son.

Large numbers of young men have joined the
native contingent as officers. Our natives are
being drilled, armed and clad as soldiers. I met
about 500 of the raw material with their weapons,
and about twenty-five of them on horseback. As
they marched along they chanted a low monotonous
chant, which was very affecting. I only saw one
whom I knew, and I gave him a hearty grasp of
the hand as I passed.

I had up all the men (of Springvale), and read
to them the award and letter to Ketchwayo.
"Friday" gave the people the sense. He was very
grave ; he told me afterwards that he had ten
brothers in Zululand, all in the army. Most of
our people are Zulus.

January 12th.—Our troops invaded the country
of the Amazulu in three columns. Special prayer
for peace and protection put forth by the Bishop.
All along I have strongly approved of our great
warlike preparations. Quite as strongly, however,
have I deprecated the invasion of the Zulu country,
because we all knew that it laid us open to a

counter-invasion threatened by Ketchwayo, and we were not prepared for it at all.

24th.—A most alarming telegram arrived to report that two large bodies of Zulus, having got to the rear of the invading armies, were trying to cross the Tugela, to sweep through Natal by order of the King.

25th.—Very anxious about the news, knowing the horrible mode of Zulu warfare ; lay awake, picturing the horrors of such a murderous and lustful raid, and determined, if possible, to place my loved ones on board ship.

26th.—Another alarming message from the magistrate, mentioning the Ixopo as the rallying place and laager. Most deeply depressed that now for the first time we were in danger, and that when our troops were so numerous, and the Governor and General both here. I was never afraid before ; I should not be so now, if our troops were defending us here in Natal.

27th.—Most terrible news. Two colonels of the British army, a number of officers, and 600 of the 1–24th, volunteers, and mounted police killed. Colonel Durnford's column cut to pieces (500 natives killed), and baggage-waggons taken; the General being within a short distance, but arriving too late to help his comrades, or to punish the Amazulu who made off with their booty. Passed a sleepless night.

28*th*.—Told the people the sad news after morning prayer, as I have done all along. It prevents idle rumours. Wept bitter tears over those brave men who stood their ground and fell nobly, doing their duty, with vain regrets mingling with my sorrowing tears, that the General should ever have parted company with them, and thus exposed them to this murderous onslaught. Oh! what a terrible loss! Oh! how fearful the consequences that may ensue if the God of Battles do not take compassion on us, and turn the tide in our favour, after so signal a defeat. One hundred waggons with their oxen and military stores, and 1,000 Martini-Henri rifles, are said to have fallen into the enemy's hands.

The arrival of the General in Pietermaritzburg to consult with Sir Bartle Frere, marks the importance of the crisis. May it please our gracious Father to protect those that are left, viz. the brave Colonel Pearson's column, and the other column of Colonel Wood's; for we all fear lest the fierce and savage Amazulu, flushed with victory, and thirsting for blood, may concentrate upon these columns a

still more overwhelming force. God has visited our
colony with a terrible chastisement.

When I was in Pietermaritzburg, I saw the
Carbiniers muster to escort Sir Bartle Frere, and a
gay and smart body of young gentlemen they were.
Archdeacon Barker's only son is with them.

They all fondly imagined they were volunteers
for Natal only, and for defence; but, alas! owing
to the supineness and indifference of home authorities, the General has been compelled to take our
only slender defence bodies, notably the mounted
police (a fine body), to invade an enemy's country,
and *such* an enemy.

Our policy has been to keep guns and powder
from our own loyal natives, and to allow villains
to fill Zululand with these murderous weapons.
What a mercy we were not invaded by the
Amazulu while trusting to a handful of men. Our
great distress and anxiety arise chiefly from two
sources:—1st. That we are the invaders; 2nd.
That it is a war with fierce, ruthless, sensual, and
cruel savages, who outnumber us from ten to five
to one, according as they are massed. Our great
hope is, that the God of Battles will not suffer the
heathen to prevail, though He has seen fit to
chasten us severely.

To me it is quite clear that the General was too far away from his camp ; that the defenders of the camp were much too scattered and unprotected by any such temporary defence as the Dutch would certainly have adopted. But both these circumstances, viz. the distance of the General from his tent (where was flying the Union Jack), and the reckless bravery of Colonel Durnford in going out to meet the foe, only prove that neither of these men could possibly have really understood the desperate bravery of the Amazulu warriors, as they pour forth their thousands headlong on the foe, sworn to conquer or to die.

Nor can it be possible for any man, in a few short months, to master all that is required, either in a statesman or a soldier, to grapple with the great difficulties which are involved in a conflict with the most powerful nation ever known in South Africa !

February 6th, 1879.—A most terrific thunderstorm. The young people never remember such a storm, One native girl said she thought it was the last day, and that the Lord had come.

South Africa has reached its crisis, and its old temporizing policy has gone for ever. But oh, how sad it is to think that so great a sacrifice as that at Isandhlwana was needed to rouse the authorities to a sense of the imminent danger of our position. Our chastisement has been sharp, sudden, and severe. Now let us hope that the doom of the Zulu dynasty is sealed.

Ketchwayo has been fomenting a spirit of revolt throughout South Africa. Let us hope that his accursed system of military despotism and enforced celibacy (entailing nameless horrors) is now tottering to its fall, to make way for justice and peace. Ketchwayo is said to have built a new kraal, and named it "Mayezekanye," *i.e.* "Let him come, then," daring the foe to invade him—defying the enemy. I hope he will wait till he does come, and not invade us.

February 9th.—Took the usual services, and preached in Zulu to the natives on the war. Ketchwayo was the wolf about to come down on the fold ; our brave men stopped him, and laid down their lives for us.

10th.—Glorious is the country now but for the curse of war. It is midsummer, verging on autumn ; grapes and peaches are ripe, and we have vegetables in abundance ; cool weather for the season, and rain in plenty. God grant that our troops in the country of the Amazulu may not be fever-stricken, for it is the season for fever there.

11th.—The Connaught Rangers arrived from King Williamstown, thank God. Our letters have not arrived, to the great disappointment of the whole neighbourhood, as we are still very anxious about the war. Schools, &c. going on as usual. Natives rather excited. Post-office messenger arrived at 4.15 P.M., having walked forty miles or so to rectify the mistake. He arrived only at midnight the day before. I praised him very much, and gave him three shillings.

March 2nd.—Only just well enough to take the service. The heat was burning. One of the native women fainted.

3rd.—Our natives are now being called out to serve in the war. One of them danced with delight at the idea. I gave this gallant warrior a shirt for the occasion, as he was a naked outsider. I have been able thus to cover all the outsiders who have come to me. One of them had the honesty to come in his shirt and report himself as not being wanted at the front. Our people at home might taken pattern from the honesty of these poor heathens. A special messenger arrived from the Captain of the Ixopo Rifles, asking me if I would sell my horses. Next day he came himself with six well-dressed native servants. He

bought one of the horses, and immediately left for
the front, where he has taken the command of 500
mounted natives, who bring their own horses and
who are clothed and armed with guns by Government, and receive 2s. 6d. a-day. The Captain,
who leaves behind some 10,000 sheep and as many
acres of land, and some 500 head of fine cattle, is
accompanied by his brother-in-law, who leaves a
young wife and two little ones, and flocks and
herds.   This will show how eager the colonists are
to retrieve the losses of Isandhlwana.

March 7th.—My son shot a splendid bird—
the bustard. It measured full six feet from tip to
tip of its wings, and stood nearly four feet high.
It is a game bird of the size of a large turkey, and
has the flavour of the grouse. The Dutch call it
the pauw (pavo), and the natives iseme.

We have now flowering in the garden near the
house a splendid plant of the South American aloe
or agave species; the leaves are seven feet long,
spiked, and straight as a dart ; the flowering stem
has shot up like a giant asparagus from thirty to
forty feet high. Lateral branches from this stem
are covered with snowdrop-looking flowers, of
which there are some 200 on each branch, and some
3,000 or more on the plant. It shoots up thus

suddenly once in a lifetime, like the mast of a
ship, and then, after seeding with olive-like seed
pods, it heels over top-heavy, or rather overcrowded
with sail, with the first strong wind, uprooting
itself and giving place to its offspring, the scions at
its roots.   We have never seen any plant so
magnificent.

This is the second that has flowered this year,
and we have never seen them flower before.   Of
the common American aloe we have myriads, and
use them for fences round the gardens, fields,
and churchyard, but this plant has not flowered
since we came six years ago.

March 16*th*.—This evening our neighbour, M.
was brought here by the natives to be doctored and
nursed.   Poor fellow!   A few weeks ago he went
to the coast to try to raise an Indian contingent,
and in returning narrowly escaped being drowned
in the flooded Nonoti, being dragged under by the
fording chain.   The other day he went to fish in
the river Umtungwane, and was in the act of
flinging a dynamite cartridge into the water when it
exploded and shattered the thumb and two fingers
and palm of his right hand.   We were afraid of
tetanus, and sent forty miles south and fifty miles
north for surgeons, but none would come.   Captain

Trevor rode this eighty miles between 12 noon and
6 next day. No doctor arriving, Mrs. Jenkinson
has done the surgical work and dressing night and
day for a week. Reinforcements are now arriving
daily, and it will be strange indeed if the Amazulu
be not conquered soon. Their subjugation has
cost us dear. Another convoy has been surprised
and cut up at the river Intombi, near Luneburg.
A Basuto chief Moirosi has been rebelling also,
and a force has been sent to prevent him joining
Ketchwayo. Uham, or Ham, the brother of
Ketchwayo, a large territorial chief, has surrendered.
This, I hope, will *divide the nation*. Mr. C.
Johnson, missionary to Hlubi, and his Basuto, gave
me, at my request, a description of the battle of
Isandhlwana from a Basuto point of view. The
Abesutu mounted men under the Natal chief
Hlubi were all present in the action under
Colonel Durnford. They say they went out to
meet the foe, and that the colonel sent for a company of soldiers to come out too ; that when this
company had fired off all their cartridges, they were
sent back and another company called out. Mean-
while the Amazulu came swarming over the hills
like bees. Firing at them was of little avail ; it
was like firing at the blades of grass. The Basuto

and other cavalry exhausted their ammunition far away from the camp, which was by this time in full possession of the enemy. Colonel Durnford fell; George Shepstone, captain of the mounted natives of Natal (son of Sir T. Shepstone) went to the rescue, and he fell too. Then the Basuto, being well mounted, fled from the field, and escaped with the loss of seventy horses and only one man. The Basuto attribute their escape to the prayers of their missionary and people at St. Augustine's. There were two brothers Tarboton, in the Carbiniers; one was killed, the other fled and crossed the Buffalo in company with Barker, son of the Archdeacon; neither of them could swim, but their horses carried them across.

I afterwards received a letter from Archdeacon Barker on this subject. He wrote saying, " My son, Walwyn, is quite safe, and was one of seven who escaped from the battle. He was pursued for twelve miles. Zulus supposed to be friendly turned against him in the drift (Rorke's drift or ford) which he had to swim. His description of the battle is heartrending. Our Father must have been his shield and protector. Verily the whole land mourneth; but let us not cast blame, rather let us acknowledge that God has permitted it for a wise purpose—to show us, perhaps, that the battle is the Lord's. We have, perhaps, been too self-confident, and, as success invariably attends our arms, have been lifted up, and therefore needed this reverse." There can be no doubt that the power of the Amazulu was as much under-rated at first as it is over-rated now. A decisive battle will be fought, probably in a few days, between the Tugela river and Etchowe. It is quite possible the day may go against us. Two heathen men came asking for news. I gave them an account of the war, and showed them a globe to explain to them how great the world was, and how wide was the sway of our Queen. I finished by telling them how great the Creator must be, and how we should pray for peace. I feel bound to tell all such inquirers that the invasion of the country of the Amazulu was no concern of mine, and that I am greatly distressed by it, though I am quite aware that a strong force was necessary to guard the colony. Our natives have a strong feeling that Somseu is at the bottom of this war. They connect it with Sir T. Shepstone's annexation of the Transvaal and the war with Sekukuni. Ketchwayo was doubtless furious at being outwitted by the crafty Somseu, as he is now mad with rage and vexation at being bearded in his den.   The Zulu Lion has inflicted a deadly wound in his turn; God grant that he may now be turned away from us, and that the British Lion may gain a decisive victory over him and break his power for ever.   This war was more for the Transvaal than for us here in Natal.   Many natives come for war news; they seem to be loyal. One poor fellow came at dawn this morning for a shirt, saying he had been called to fight.

I subjoin a summary of this horrid war from my point of view.

It was remarked that in the Queen's Speech South Africa was not even named, although Sir Bartle Frere was here in Natal, and the Commander-in-Chief, and a terrible war was imminent. Our synod took place in December 1878, and just after this appeared the Zulu award and ultimatum. On arriving at Springvale I called together all the men (Zulus chiefly) and read them this award. It took two hours to read and explain in the Zulu tongue.   Two matters struck me in this ultimatum. First, the quiet assumption of superiority and the request that Ketchwayo would disband his army. The Zulu king refused, of course, and then our troops invaded Zululand, crossing the river Tugela on the 12th of January 1879.   I was greatly troubled at this and spoke against it at the time, my argument being that if Ketchwayo had really wished to invade Natal he might easily have done so time after time. However, all is over now. The die was cast and our own utterly defenceless state was laid bare to the remorseless fury of the savage Zulu. The army crossed in four columns —Colonel Wood's from the north-west, Colonel Glyn's from Rorke's drift, Colonel Durnford's attached to Colonel Glyn's was central, and Colonel Pearson's was near the sea, sixty miles north of Port Natal. I myself trembled for the result. On the 24th came the terrible news that Colonel Durnford's column had been cut up, and that the Zulus, having killed 1,000 men, were about to sweep through Natal. A terrible panic ensued throughout the colony. A desperate stand was made by Lieutenants Chard and Bromhead, and the Zulu force was driven back with the loss of some hundreds. A month has passed away since that fatal day, and still we feel that it is of God's mercy that we are not consumed. I quite believe that nothing happens by chance, and that our defeat was simply a chastisement, for what I will not pretend to say. Our invasion of Zululand was at least premature. It was a cruel thing to lay us open suddenly to an invasion of ruthless barbarians, without giving us time to remove our helpless women and children. It is a marvel to me how graciously our Father has shielded us. The battle is the Lord's. In the enemy's country a Zulu force of twenty to one cut us off almost to a man. In this country the same force flushed with victory, yet thirty to one, was thoroughly beaten with a loss of 500 Zulus to ten British soldiers. Is not the hand of God in all this? Are there not lessons for us here? We are now gaining strength and preparing for the worst. By the middle of March active military preparations are to be resumed. Wood is harassing the foe continually. Glyn waiting and defending the border. Pearson entrenched at Etchowe (an old Norwegian missionary station thirty-five miles from the border).

March 25th.—The war which has engaged so much of our attention and absorbed our thoughts so much of late, began to turn in our favour, but not before we had suffered another defeat. Colonel Wood's cavalry surrounded on the Hlobane Mount by the Zulu army, and ninety-one white men killed, which victory emboldened the Zulus to attack Colonel Wood's camp, where, after four hours' hard fighting, they were repulsed and driven away with great loss.

April 2nd.—Complete victory by Lord Chelms-
ford at Ginginhlovu, and relief of Colonel Pearson
at Etchowe. As I had told my people that the
next battle, and that a decisive one, would be
fought between the Tugela and Etchowe, they
naturally regarded this victory as a very great one
for us. Who, however, could have foreseen and
foretold that the Zulus would have brought 20,000
to bear upon Colonel Wood, and only 21,000 upon
a much stronger force, viz. the relief column?
Our people show their sympathy with us entirely.
They seem very hard, however, and do not mourn
for the killed on both sides as we do.

On my return from a long ride of 200 miles I
took to visit St. Augustine's Mission, near the
Kahlamba mountains, I had the opportunity of
seeing the Gatling-gun battery at Howick, and
passed the Army Hospital Corps. The whole road
from Weston to Pietermaritzburg was thick with
waggons making for the front. They were without
number, but in one place my eye rested on ten, in
another twelve, in another sixteen. The Dragoons
were at Estcourt on Sunday the 4th of May.

On the 14th of June I left Springvale in a
waggon, and travelled *viâ* Umzinto and the Umkomazi to Durban. Port Natal 120 miles.

On the 21st or 22nd we reached Durban, and the following day embarked for Algoa bay on board the "Melrose." In a few days we were transferred to the splendid ship the "Conway Castle," and on the 22nd of July 1879 we landed at Plymouth, by the mercy of God.

The day after, we read in the papers the news of the battle of Ulundi, which was decisive, and which was the *end* of the Zulu war.

PART III.

Historical Notices of the Zulu Nation.

The following notices of the Zulus from original sources will be found instructive at this time.*

Mr. Charles Johnson, missionary of the S.P.G. to the Hlubi Chief of a Basuto tribe, placed over that part of Zululand in which Isandhlwana is situated, writes as follows:

" I have found out a most curious fact. When Senzangakona (Chaka's father) was chief of the Zulus (they being then but a small tribe), a Basuto tribe occupied the district, commencing at the Nquto range of mountains, or rather at the head of the Nquto range stretching all down past Isandhlwana to the Buffalo river. In fact, they took in

---

* See also "Macmillan's Magazine" for Feb. 1880, "Ketchwayo's Story of the Zulu Nation and War."

the whole of what is called Sihhayo's district and a
good deal more.   Their chief was Seka, half-cousin
to Sekukulu (spelt Sekukuni).   Senzangakona was
succeeded by Chaka, and Seka (the Basuto chief)
by Weza.   Chaka attacked Weza, and overcame
him—" ate him up."   He could not destroy all his
people, but managed to drive them north-west, or
nearly due west, into a country known as the
boundary between the Orange Free State and the
Transvaal.   There they multiplied fast, and were
joined by other Basuto from the neighbouring
tribes, until they became very powerful.   But a
civil war broke out; at the same time they were
attacked by Korannas, helped by some Dutch
settlers.   By this they were broken up and
separated; their troubles were many and great.
One portion took refuge in Natal under Umbunda
(Hlubi's father), and so it happens that Hlubi and
his people are simply returning to the homes of
their fathers.   'Amanxiwa ya kwabo.'   They take
pride in pointing out a few piled-up stones, and
saying ' our fathers' homesteads.' "

Lewis Grout, American missionary, 1859, says:
" We find the Amazulu a small tribe living on the
Umfolosi and neighbouring rivers, between the
28th and 29th degrees south latitude, and between

the 31st degree east longitude and the Indian Ocean.

" They are reported to have come down at some former period from a more inland region on the west and north-west.

" The line of Zulu chiefs is Umpande, who succeeded his brother Dingane, who succeeded his brother Chaka, son of Usenzangakona, son of Jama, son of Umakeba, who was the son of Upunga.

" Chaka was born about the year 1787. His father was rich in wives and children, having some twenty-five or thirty of the former, and no one knows how many of the latter.

" Between him and one of his wives, Umnandi (the Sweet One), the mother of Chaka, there arose some cause of bitterness. In consequence of this difference between husband and wife, the mother took the boy Chaka and fled, first to the Amakwabe, and then to the Amatetwa, whose chief at that time was Udingiswayo.

" The Amatetwa, reported to have come down along the coast from the north-east at a former period, were now a powerful tribe, living neighbours to the Amazulu.

" Udingiswayo gave Chaka and his mother to the

care] of Ungomana, an Induna, or chief councillor of his tribe."

Theal, " History of South Africa " :—" At this time the Zulu tribe was small and tributary to the Amatetwa. Udingiswayo, in his younger days, had fled to the Cape Colony, and remained there long enough to learn the art of training men to war, the organization of an army. On the death of his father, Jobe, he returned home and was made chief. He formed his men into regiments and made war upon his neighbours.

" The Zulu refugee became a private soldier in one of Udingiswayo's regiments, from which position he raised himself to a situation of command.

" When Senzengakona died, Chaka was nominated to the chieftainship of the Amazulu.

" On the death of Udingiswayo, the united army of the Amatetwa and Amazulu raised Chaka to supreme power."

Grout goes on to say : " At the head of a tribe whose very name (from *izulu*, heaven) is equivalent to the celestials, now increased in numbers, strength, and courage, by a voluntary alliance with another powerful tribe ; himself an ambitious man, of royal blood, in the prime of life, already adored as of more than human origin, panting for forays, victory, and plunder, Chaka sallied forth in person at the head of his warriors, soon conquered the tribe against which his aid had been asked, and added them to his own tribe. Pursuing this policy, he conquered one tribe after another, located them here and there among his own people, taking care so to distribute, guard, and govern them as to hold them in the most complete awe and subordination to himself. It this way he seems to have gone on five or six years without much interruption, increasing the number of his subjects and tributaries, the strength of his army, and the extent of his dominions, so that in 1822 his conquering power was felt from the Umzimvubu, or St. John's, on the south-west, to Inhambane on the north-east, and from the sea-coast inland, across at least half the continent of Africa."

Theal (chap. xxxix.), 1877, says : " Sixty years ago the country between the Limpopo and the Vaal was inhabited by Bechuana ; only a chain of mountains lay between them and the countries ravaged by Chaka. Over that chain came Umsilikazi with an army of Zulu warriors. He had been one of Chaka's generals, but he had offended him and was compelled to flee for his life. The

Bechuana looked with dismay upon the athletic
forms of the Matabele, as they called the invaders.
The clans fled in terror; those that attempted to
resist were exterminated. The land was depopulated. Then the Boers crossed the Vaal. Umsilikazi
stood at bay and put forth all his strength in vain;
he was driven far beyond the Limpopo to a tract
of country near the Zambesi."

Moffat (chap. xxx.) says: " In 1829 two traders
journeyed into the interior for the purpose of
shooting elephants. Hearing that a tribe possessing
much cattle lived at some distance eastward, they
proceeded thither, and were received in a friendly
manner by Moselekatse, the king of that division
of Zulus called Abaka, or Matabele. He is called
Uselekas, or Umsiligas, by the Zulus. When a
youth his father was chief of an independent tribe.
He took refuge under the sceptre of Chaka.
Moselekatse was placed at the head of a marauding
expedition, which made dreadful havoc among the
northern tribes; but instead of giving up the whole
of the spoils, he made a reserve for himself. This
reaching the ears of Chaka, he resolved to annihilate
so daring an aggressor.

" Moselekatse escaped, and rushed onward to the
north. Commandoes of Chaka had made frightful

havoc among the Bakones; but these were as
nothing compared with the final overthrow of these
tribes by the arms of Moselekatse. His destructive career, dire as it was, must have been only
a faint transcript of the terror, desolation, and
death which extended to the utmost limits of
Chaka's arms. The Matabele were not satisfied
with simply capturing cattle, nothing less than the
entire subjugation or destruction of the vanquished
could quench their thirst for power. When they
conquered a town, the terrified inhabitants were
driven in mass to the outskirts, when the parents
and all the married women were slaughtered on the
spot.

" I had scarcely a hope that the Gospel would be
successful among the Matabele *until there should
be a revolution* in the government of a monarch
who demanded that homage which pertains to God
alone."

"Though but a follower in the footsteps of
Chaka, the career of Moselekatse formed an in-
terminable catalogue of crimes. Those who
resisted, and would not stoop to be his dogs, he
butchered. He trained the captured youth in his
own tactics, so that the majority of his army were
foreigners, but his chiefs and nobles gloried in the

descent from the Zulu dynasty. He had carried
his arms far into the tropics, where, however, he
had more than once met with his equal, and on one
occasion, of 600 warriors only a handful returned,
to be sacrificed merely because they had not conquered or fallen with their companions.

"He dipped his sword in blood and wrote his
name on lands and cities desolate.

"When I recommended a system which would
secure not only safety but plenty to his people
without the *unnatural one* of keeping up a force
of many thousands of *unmarried* warriors, he tried
to convince me that his people were happy.

"The happiness of the king and his subjects
appeared to be derived from their success in
war."

Mr. Isaacs, 1825, quoted by Bishop Colenso,
says: "The imperial residence had now changed
its name to Umbulalo, 'place of slaughter,' from
the fact of the king Chaka having recently ordered
one of his regiments with their wives and families
to be massacred."

On another occasion Mr. Isaacs witnessed the
execution of 170 boys and girls.

"During the greater part of Chaka's reign,
which lasted twenty-five years, the district of Natal

was utterly devastated and depopulated by the
continual inroads of this inhuman tyrant."

Mr. Fynn, quoted by Bishop Colenso, gives the
following account of the proceedings (which he
witnessed) on the death of Chaka's mother:—

"As soon as the death was announced the
women and the men who were present tore from
their persons every description of ornament.
Chaka now appeared before the hut in which the
body lay. For about twenty minutes he stood in a
silent mournful attitude. After two or three deep
sighs, he broke out into fanatic yells. This signal
was enough. The chiefs and people, to the number of about 15,000, commenced the most dismal
and horrible lamentations. Through the whole
night this continued, none daring to take rest, or
to refresh themselves with water. . . . The morning dawned, and before noon the number had
increased to 60,000. The cries became inde-
scribably horrible. Hundreds were lying faint
from fatigue, while the carcases of forty oxen lay
in a heap, which had been slaughtered as an
offering to the guardian spirits of the tribe. At
noon the whole force formed a circle with Chaka
in their centre, and sang the war song; at the close
Chaka ordered some men to be executed on the

spot, and the cries became more violent. No further orders were needed. The multitude commenced a general massacre. Towards the afternoon I calculated that 7,000 people had fallen in this frightful massacre. Amidst this scene I stood unharmed, and felt as if the whole universe was coming to an end. The sun again set, and Chaka now put an end to this general massacre. The cries continued till 10 o'clock the following morning, when the chief became somewhat pacified, and his subjects were permitted to take some refreshment. On the second day Chaka's mother was buried, and ten of the best-looking girls of the kraal were buried alive with her. I was told this; I was not allowed to be present. Twelve thousand men were formed into a regiment to guard the grave. About 15,000 head of cattle were set apart for their use, as offerings to the spirits of the departed queen and her ill-fated attendants.

"Hitherto the proceedings had been local. Gomani, Chaka's principal chief, proposed that no cultivation should be allowed during the following year; no milk should be used, it should be all poured on the earth; and all women, who should be found with child during the year should, with their husbands, be put to death. At the close of this speech regiments of soldiers were dispersed through the country, who massacred everyone they could find that had not been present at the general wailing.

"At the end of the year Chaka left the kraal where his mother died, and came with his whole nation and cattle to Tuguza on the Umvoti river (Natal), where he was subsequently assassinated. I started to pay him a visit, and met him on his march a few miles south of the Tugela. He told me that another lamentation was then to take place. I begged him to grant me one request. He smiled, and asked what it could possibly be? I entreated him not to allow on this occasion any of his people to be put to death. He at once called for Gomani, and laughing ' that I should plead for the life of dogs,' gave orders to him to see that none were put to death. He now advanced with his chiefs in their full war-dress. Presently Tukuza came in sight. Upon this he began to cry and sob. The whole population took up, as before, the frantic cry of their chief; with the general yelling was mingled the bellowing of 100,000 oxen.

"The next morning the purification took place.

Each regiment presented itself before Chaka, and each individual holding the gall-bladder of a slaughtered calf in his hand, sprinkled the gall over him.

" After this Gomani made another speech.

" The tribe had now lamented for a year the death of her who had now become a spirit, and who would continue to watch over Chaka's welfare; but there were nations of men, who because they had not yet been conquered, supposed that they never should be. War should be made against them, and the cattle taken should be the tears shed upon the grave of the Great Mother of earth and corn."—" Ten Weeks in Natal," p. 224.

From " A Narrative of a Journey to the Zoolu Country in South Africa," by Captain Allen F. Gardiner, R.N., undertaken in 1835 :—

" The object of my journey was to open a way whereby the ministers of the Gospel might find access to the Zoolu nation."

The ancestors of Dingane were Jama, Senzangakona, Chaka. The Umtetwa under Dingiswayo (with which Chaka was brought up) were at that period a people far more powerful than the Zoolus.

Chaka usually headed his army, but at the

period of his death they were engaged on a distant expedition against Sotchangan, ruling a country north-west of Delagoa bay.

In 1829 two of his brothers, Dingane and Umhlangana, conspired against his life, assisted by Satain a principal domestic (*inceku*, house steward). He received an assegai wound in his back. He arose and fell. His last words were, " What have I done to you, children of my father?" Although Dingane was present, it is not believed that he took an active part.

Captain Gardiner at first failed to gain leave for the missionaries to come and teach the people, the Izinduna, Umhlela, and Tambuza, being opposed to it. This, their opposition, he attributes to a prophecy of Jacob's, the interpreter to Lieutenant Fanwell, who told Chaka that a white teacher would come amongst them, that shortly after he would be joined by one or two more white men, and in course of time an army would enter his country which would subject his government, and eventually the white people would rule in his stead.

Dingane put to death Goujuana, his own brother, while Captain Gardiner was there. " When a chief falls," says he, " by the hand of the executioner all his property is confiscated, and every individual who is connected with him is put to death. An induna, who lived in a hut adjoining mine, was ordered on this revolting duty, and from his lips on his return the following account is given: The property of Goujuana was in the neighbourhood of the Tugela, and thither he was sent with thirty men to destroy the entire population of ten villages (kraals). On reaching the first of these devoted places he entered with one man only, to avoid suspicion; in the course of the evening one or two more dropped in, until the whole had arrived. He then informed the principal men that he had a message to deliver from the king. While offering them snuff and apparently on the most friendly terms, each of the induna's party rose and stabbed his fellow with an assegai; the houses were instantly fired, and the women and children butchered The same horrors were perpetrated at each of the remaining villages. It is truly lamentable to reflect on the numbers of cold-blooded murders which are thus systematically occurring in these habitations of cruelty."

He mentions an unsuccessful raid into the territories of Umselikazi, of whom he says, " This chieftain is of Zulu origin, his people are the same, but during the reign of Chaka a separation was made.

" During the reign of Chaka no soldier was permitted to marry until he had distinguished himself in war"; there is no limit, however, to the number of their concubines. The example of Chaka and Dingane has tended to uphold this baneful system.

" Neither Chaka nor Dingane ever allowed that they had any children. On one occasion an infant was presented to Chaka; the 'hyena man' instantly seized his own child and with one blow deprived it of life. This horrid deed was only surpassed by the immediate murder of the agonized mother."

Captain Gardiner, on a second visit, obtained the consent of Dingane to send missionaries. The Church Missionary Society, to whom application for succour was made, accepted the two stations of Berea (Durban) and Culoola (Zululand) as well as the management of the Zulu Mission in future."

Port Natal, 23rd June 1835.—" In consequence of the exterminating wars of Chaka, late King of the Zoolus, and other causes, the whole country included between the Umzimkoolu and Tugela rivers is now unoccupied by its original possessors, and, with very few exceptions, is totally uninhabited. Numbers of natives (about 3,000) have entered this settlement for protection.

" The natives at Port Natal are, almost to a man, refugees from the Zoolu nation, goaded by a rigorous government to desert for protection to our settlement."

" In August 1837 the Rev. F. Owen, with his wife and sister, landed at Port Natal, as the first missionaries of the Church of England to the Zulu Kafirs. In company with Captain Gardiner, Mr. Owen paid his first visit to Dingane, and preached a sermon before him on the leading truths of revelation, 6th August 1837."—" Missionary Register."

The following are extracts from the journal of the Rev. Francis Owen taken from the "Missionary Register," September 1838:—

" *August 5th*, 1837.—Commenced my journey yesterday into the interior of the Zoolah country, for the purpose of visiting the Chief Dingane. Meeting with Mr. Grote, an American missionary, I was by him directed to the lovely spot which Captain Gardiner has fixed upon for his dwelling, near the mouth of the Umtomgata. On the south bank of the Tugela were several villages, lately peopled by a tribe of Zoolahs called Amapiesi, or Hyena people, who shortly before our arrival fled to Port Natal, having suspected Dingane of some design upon them.

" *August* 16*th*, 1837.—On the other side of the Tugela a beautifully wooded country was now exchanged for naked hills. We passed Clomanthleen Nyanu; this being the first Zoolah town I had seen, I felt much interested. In the midst of the town is a large vacant area, surrounded by a fence; on the outside of this fence, which is circular, the huts are disposed in rows; an outer fence incloses the whole town. A segment of the circular town, at that part of it which is opposite to the principal entrance, is cut off by a fence; and in this segment, which is called the isigorthlo, are several huts, appropriated to distinguished personages : only the military towns, or barracks, have these isigorthlos. A regiment is stationed at each town, under several indunas. The huts at this town were nearly all empty, the regiment being engaged in the war with Umselekaz.

"*August* 17*th*.—Rode forward to Congella, passing Intonella, a large military town on the road. Congella is the second capital of the Zoolah nation, where the King spends the great part of the year.

Dingane having assigned this place to Captain Gardiner for a mission station, we walked about to look for a site, which was found about two miles from the town.

"*August* 18*th and* 19*th.*—On leaving Congella, the road descends into the vale of the Umthlatoosi; after crossing which stream, it ascends some high mountains which form a magnificent sight from Congella. The King being now at Nobamba, his birthplace, we proceeded toward that town. The whole country thereabout is very populous, large towns being seen in every direction. On our arrival, Dingane sent for us; he was seated inside his isigorthlo; he began by asking Captain Gardiner many questions. . . .

" *August* 20*th, Lord's day.*—Sent to request the King to give me permission to preach publicly to his people. This was granted.

" *August* 21*st.*—Dingane sent for us early this morning. He asked me why I was in such a hurry to teach his people ? I said that life was short. He asked how that could be, as, according to me, we were all to wake again. He sent forth his servants, who, with loud voices, called all the men of the town together. When they were all seated, to the number of 300, he told me that I might

now preach the same words to them which I had
spoken yesterday, and begged me to go forward
and stand in the midst of them. Dingane was not
attentive. He made sport with a blind man, whom
he bade go and look for something. The poor
fellow stumbled about, ran against me, and fell
over my auditory. I felt grieved. . . .

"*August* 28*th.*—Arrived at *Berea* (Durban). The
distance from Port Natal to Unkunkinglove is about
150 miles.

" *September* 10*th, Lord's day.*—I was much pleased
at the readinsss of the natives to be taught the
Word of God.

"*September* 14*th.*—Leave Berea for Unkunkinglove the capital.

"*September* 18*th.*—Arrived at Umtomgata (Ton-
gaat?) on a visit to our friends, Captain and Mrs.
Gardiner, at Ambanati. Captain Gardiner had set
off to the Zoolah country, Dingane having sent for
him on the occasion of the return of his army from
Umsilikazi's country, where they had gone for the
sake of plunder. Umsilikazi's father was conquered by one of the Zoolah kings, and afterwards
became an independent and powerful chief. His
country lies to the north-west of the Zulus. Umsilikazi had been vanquished and fled for his life.

" 23*rd.*—Proceeded onward to the Tugela. The inhabitants of the villages freely brought us milk, having been directed by the King to show this hospitality to strangers. The distance of the Tugela from Natal is about sixty miles.

" *September* 25*th.*—Crossed the river and arrived at Nginani (' I am with you '), a settlement of the American missionaries established a twelvemonth.

"*September* 30*th.*—Across the river Umlalasi, the face of the country changes ; it reminds me now of the peak ; heat excessive, thermometer at blood-heat.

" *October* 8*th,* *Lord's day.*—Observed a dense mass of people advancing down the slope from the town (Ukayakanina). The men came foremost, the women remained behind. My interpreter and I sat down on chairs between the men and the women. I gave them a short account of the Creation, the Covenant of Life. On mentioning the name of our Blessed Lord, the induna repeated it several times, asking me if this was God, &c.

"*October*10*th,*1837.—Arrived at Unkunkinglove. Dingaan sent word that we were to come to the isigorthlo. He seemed mightily pleased. He peeped into my waggon, and spying Mrs. and Miss Owen, begged them to come out. Next he called for my interpreter, wife and children, and surveyed them with minute attention and silent pleasure.

"*October* 11*th*.—Dingaen sent for me. Three men were sitting on the ground before him. These, he told me, were his three head indunas, Umthlella, Tambooza, and Mavuti, who had commanded the army which had gone out against Umsilikazi. Tambooza told me to sit down. As the conversation began about Umsilikazi, I asked Dingaen whether many of his people had been killed in the war? He said, not more than ten; but this I could not believe, as the number of huts, mats, &c. which had been burned indicated many more.

"*October* 12*th*.—Dingaen sent for me to see his female servants, at least 500, ornamented with beads, who were summoned forth to sing. . . . when the King's women, ninety in number, advanced, richly attired with beads and brass rings. These ladies being too unwieldy, sat as they sang. They seemed to be worked up to a frenzy. Dingaen then said he would show me some of Umsilikazi's oxen. I said I hoped he would not retaliate on his enemy any more. I asked him where the Zoolu nation originally came from? He said they had always lived here. I asked him the name of the first king? He said Uzulu, and that he had begun to conquer the tribes hereabout, and that the grave I saw was that of his son.

"*October* 13*th*, 1837.—Dingaen sent the boys early this morning, but the man who brought them had directions to bring me and the children to Unkunkinglove, as the King wished to see how I taught them.

" *October* 23*rd*.—Dingaen sent for me to open a parcel. There was Captain Gardiner's narrative of his journey to this country in it. I began to be frightened lest Dingaen should open the book and see his own likeness. He asked to see the great book. He took the book and examined all the pictures, which highly amused him.

" *October* 26*th*, 1837.—I read a letter to Dingaen, which he had received from the Dutch Boors, who have lately left the colony (Cape Colony), expressing their desire for peace, and a good understanding with the Zoolu nation ; to effect which, it was their wish to have, by means of their chief head, a personal interview with Dingaen, who would at the same time also arrange with Dingaen, the place of their future residence, which is to be in some part of the uninhabited country adjoining the Zulu territories. The letter was dated from Port Natal, and signed by the chief of the Boors. Their party were dispersed in various parts of the country. The letter also stated the cause of their rupture with Umsilikazi, Dingaen's great foe, who, by means of the Boors and Zulus, is now said to be utterly vanquished.

"*October* 27*th*.—Dingaen sent for me to read the letter to Umhlela. Showed him the Encyclopedia.

"28*th*.—Dingaen sent to-day for English garments to clothe his people with. The children continue to attend regularly once or twice a day.

"31*st*.—Dingaen sent for me soon after 5 A.M. with directions to bring pen, ink, and paper. He told me the way in which the witches went to work. He said they went out in the dead of the night, carrying a cat, that they sent this cat into the house of the person whom they meant to bewitch. The cat brought out a bit of hair, or something else, which the witch deposited under the floor of her house, and that in consequence the object of her malice in due time fell sick. There were five animals thus used: the cat, the wolf, the panther, the jackal, and the owl. I said I hoped that now missionaries had come there would be an end of witchcraft. He said, ' Why they will not be afraid of you; they are not even afraid of the smellers-out' (*izinyanya zokubula*) diviners.

" *November* 3*rd*, 1837.—Dingaen sent for me to write a letter to Captain Gardiner, to request him to come and advise with the King respecting the territory to be assigned to the Boors. The letter being written, Dingaen began more than ever to admire the art of writing; and asked, as he had done a thousand times, whether he should ever be able to learn it. He then began to read.

" *November* 4*th.*—Intense cold prevented the children from assembling. The King sent for me to read another letter which he had received from the Dutch. It was written in Dutch, a language I do not understand. But I observed that the Dutch would be here the day after to-morrow. Dingaen's hut was very warm ; his house does great honour to native architecture. It is very spacious, lofty, and exquisitely neat ; the floor is as bright as polished marble ; a fireplace very tastily devised, and the roof formed of sticks (rods), closely compacted together. It is supported by twenty-one posts which are covered with beads of various colours.

" *November* 5*th*, 1837, *Lord's day.*—Dingaen sent early to say that, as it was so cold, they would not be able to attend divine service. In the afternoon the Dutch arrived. Dingaen sent for me to come

and see them. I went. The Dutch expressed
their disappointment that they did not arrive in
time for service. The deputation consisted of four
persons. When I got home I saw Dingaen making
an exhibition of his cattle. The herd consists of
white-back oxen only, but it was without number.

"*November* 6*th*, 1837.—Dingane afforded amusement to the Dutch by collecting a large body of
men to dance. The Governor, Mr. Retief, dined
with us. Dingane told him that pleasure must
take precedence of business. The indunas, he
said, had been asking the King to go once more
against Umsilikazi, to bring his head. We were
much pleased with the frank and open manner of
our guest.

"*November* 7*th*.—Dingane sent for me to witness
the festivities in honour of the Dutch. One whole
regiment of young men who have not a ring on
their head were summoned to exhibit their skill in
military exercises. The first act was a representa-
tion of the manner in which the Zulus commence
a battle. The regiment divided into companies,
each soldier having a stick in each hand, or the
horn or the bone of some beast, for very few had
their shields and no one his spear, with a sort of
double quick march, and performed various evolu-

tions, exciting themselves to the supposed combat by some note of their voice, and by raising their sticks in the air. On a sudden they gave a whistle, and forming into one large company, they rushed furiously as if to a charge down the open area of the town, whistling as they ran. Some who had shields, leaping aloft and kicking their shields, cried out, ' We are as hard as stones; nothing shall hurt us!' Presently the military divided into two parts, when they made a tremendous rush, as if engaging each other in close conflict. The Zulus do not throw their spears as other tribes do, but come to close quarters. After this they formed a large semicircle, in which they stood very thick and deep, their numbers being beyond count, and began to sing and dance. When the review was over another party began to assemble.

"*November* 20*th*.—Commenced turning Psalm xix. into Zulu.

" 26*th*, *Lord's Day*.—The most painful day since the commencement of the mission. The King sent a message saying that he was much displeased ; he expected the missionaries to instruct him in what he most wanted to know—alluding to fire-arms. Therefore, I might come and preach, but for the last time. When we arrived

(Dr. Wilson accompanied me), Dingane was sitting,
as usual, outside the fence of his isigorthlo, the men
of the town sitting at some distance ready to begin
their breakfast, consisting of bowls of native beer.
Instead of giving thanks to the Father of all
mercies, these men praise the King for this bounty,
shaking their fingers in the air and making a
hissing sound, and shouting ' Bayete ! Our
Father!' Dingane said the white people were not
one with him. I would not lend him a bullet-
mould ; he was offended. I began to preach
by telling them that there was a great Chief
above the sky ; we are all sinners before Him ;
our souls must be *washed*. Now contradiction
began, which lasted two hours. The indunas
and the King were the chief objectors. The
subject was treated with scorn. ' Away ! it is all
a lie !' I persisted. They asked how Jesus Christ
was killed. Dingane then asked if it was God that
died. After a great deal more combat, they told
me that I need not speak to them any more about
the Resurrection, for they would not believe it, and
to " say no more about the dead, leave them where
they are ; go to the sick and keep them from
dying," &c. Dingane at length told me that the
sun was hot, and that I must tell him when I had

done. I said I had only one question to ask:
' Did they not believe that the spirits of their
ancestors survived their bodies ? ' He said, ' All
they believed about them was this, that when a
person was sick the doctor was consulted, who
sometimes said that the spirit of the sick man's
father had caused the sickness, and advised the sick
man to appease the father's spirit with a bullock,
and after this he sometimes got better."

" *November* 27*th*.—Dingane sent for me to read a
letter he had received from Captain Gardiner.

" 28*th*–30*th*.—Arrival at the American Missionary
Station on the banks of the Umhlatoosi.

" *December* 7*th*.—Dingane sent early for me to
read some letters from Retief. In allusion to the
ruin of the chief Umsilikazi, Retief observed that
his punishment was brought upon him by the
righteous judgment of God."

" *December* 14*th*.—Dingane sent for me to write
to Captain Gardiner.

" Messengers arrived from Gardiner to inform us
of some secret machinations of Dingane in which
the safety of ourselves and all the white people was
concerned.

" *December* 19*th*.—The Umkunkinglove regiment
is collecting to celebrate the feast of the first-fruits.

"*December* 29*th*, 1837, *to January* 1*st*, 1838.—
Executions.   Victims to barbarous severity.

"*January* 2*nd*.—Letter informed Dingane that
the Boors had sent another commander against
Umsilikazi, had slain 500 of his people, and captured
3,000 head of cattle.   It informed him that they were
going to retake Dingane's cattle from the Basuto.

"*February* 2*nd*.—Dingane sent for me to write a
letter to Retief, who, with a party of Boors, is now
on his way to the Zoolu capital.   He said he was
content because he had got his cattle again.   He
requested the chief of the Boors would send to all
his people and order them to come up to the
capital with him, but without their horses.   He
promised to gather all his army, to sing and dance
in the presence of the Dutch, who, he desired, would
also dance.

"*February* 3*rd*.—Large parties of Zoolus, in their
war dress, entered the town.   The Boors entered
the town on horseback, with their guns, about sixty.
The Boors showed Dingane the way in which they
danced on horseback by making a sham charge at
one another, making the air resound with their
guns.   This was something which the Zulu chief
had never witnessed.   In their turn the Zulus
exhibited their agility in dancing.

" About noon I paid a visit to Retief. The answer which he gave to Dingane, when he *demanded* the *guns* and horses, was, to show the messenger his grey hairs, and bid him tell his master that he was not dealing with a child.

" *February 4th, Lord's Day.*—With the sun, singing and dancing commenced.

" *February 6th.*—A dreadful day in the annals of the mission ; I shudder to give an account of it.

" Dingane sent to tell me not to be frightened, as he was going to kill the Boors. The reason assigned was that they were going to kill him. . . My attention was directed to the blood-stained hill where executions take place, ' There, they are killing the Boors.' I turned my eyes, and beheld an immense multitude on the hill ; about nine or ten Zulus to each Boor were dragging their helpless unarmed victim to the fatal spot. Mrs. and Miss Owen were not more thunderstruck than myself. Many of the Boors had children with them, some under eleven years of age ; these were all butchered. The number slain must have been nearer a hundred than sixty. Thermometer 101°.

" *February 8th.*—Troops of warriors have been seen going to-day to join the army which has gone out against the Boors.

"¡9th.—The angel of death has been lately crying with a loud voice to all the fowls that fly in the midst of heaven, ' Come and gather yourselves together!' Numerous birds of prey flying over the hill whitened with the bones of men. The King sent for my interpreter soon after his arrival, and gave him a plausible account of the late unhappy affair. He said that if he had not despatched the Boors, they would have fired at him and his people before they left; and that when their guns were examined they were all found loaded with ball. The perfidious tyrant gave the following account of the manner in which they had been seized. He invited them all into the cattle-fold to take leave of him; his people were then ordered to dance, and forming themselves, as usual, into a half-moon, they came nearer and nearer to the Boors, till he gave the command to lay hold of the unsuspecting victims of his jealousy. Having duly reflected on our present situation, I determined to inform Dingane of my intentions. As war is inevitable we are not secure in this place. We see a storm coming. I took a present of red cloth to the chief, with which he was much pleased. I then said I was going (to leave) on account of the troubles that were coming. He told me to tell him what was in

my heart. ' Was I leaving,' he asked ' on account
of the Boors ? ' I said, ' That that *was* my
reason, for I feared there would be war.' He
asked, ' What war ? ' I said, ' Between his
nation and the Amabunu ' (Dutch). He was
grave ; he said he would wish me a pleasant
journey. I told him I hoped to return. I fancy
he anticipated my departure after his sad and
wicked conduct.

" *February* 10*th*.—The Chief sent for me to tell
me the words I was to speak at Port Natal. On
my arrival he called several of his great indunas
about him, and began to acquaint them with my
determination of leaving, saying he did not know
the reason, whether it was that I was fretting for
the Boors, or for some other cause. His manner
became more vehement. He referred to our native
servants. We praised God, he said, but reviled
him. He despatched messengers for the servants.
They returned with the two girls and the boy.
One of the girls said that we called him (Dingane),
an evil doer, a murderer, and a rogue, &c.

" The King then said to his indunas, ' You hear
what they say.' "

Extracts from a letter of the Rev. F. Owen,
Port Natal :—

Port Natal, March 16*th.*—After the massacre. —
" Dingane immediately sent out a large army to
attack the camp (of the Boors).   The account
brought by a Natal resident who was with the Dutch
when this attack was made, states that 250 of the
Boors, including women and children, were slain.
They were surprised at break of day on 16th
February.   The rest, rallying, defended themselves;
and the Zulus, flying, were pursued with dreadful
slaughter, at least 500 men killed.   You can conceive our feelings when we were first informed of the
massacre of the Boors, and when we saw the army
go out to attack the camp.   I could no longer stay
with the despot, but the same week took my leave of
him.   I was charged with condemning his conduct
in killing the Dutch."

Bishop Colenso, in his "Historical Sketch," p. xx.,
says, " Immediately after this horrible massacre
ten regiments of the King's soldiers had been sent
forth to attack the emigrant farmers.   The Zulu
forces fell upon the party of Retief encamped near
Weenen (weeping) ; men, women, and children
were butchered.   The alarm spread; the farmers
were able to form laagers.   The Zulus were re-
pelled by well-directed firing from these laagers,
but they pressed on till at last they were driven

back. The scenes left behind were horrible beyond description.

" Two desperate efforts were made to avenge upon the Zulu king the death of Retief and his party. A Dutch commando of 300 fighting men, under Pieter Uys, marched up into his country and boldly attacked his forces, but were obliged to retire, leaving their leader dead. A still more terrible disaster befel another expedition from Port Natal. Almost every European was killed and multitudes of natives, while the furious troops of Dingaan now ranged freely over the country and had their fill of carnage.

" The emigrants were more successful afterwards. Dingaan's army was routed, and his capital, Umkunginghlovu, taken and destroyed; and at length, in 1840, they supported his brother Panda in rebellion against him. Dingaan was utterly routed and perished among a neighbouring tribe (Amaswazi) with whom he took refuge."

In 1856 a desperate battle was fought between Panda's sons Ketchwayo and Umbulazi, rivals. Umbulazi was defeated with great slaughter. In 1872 Ketchwayo succeeded Panda.

Livingstone, in his " Missionary Travels in South Africa," says: " From 1845 to 1849 I attached

myself to a tribe called Bakuena, the chief of
which, Sechele, was then living at a place called
Shoknane. . . . One of the difficulties with which
the mission had to contend was the vicinity of the
Boers of the Cashan mountains, or ' Magaliesberg '
(Transvaal). These Boers are not to be con-
founded with the Cape colonists, who are sober and
industrious. Those who have fled from English
law, and have been joined by every variety of bad
character, are of a very different stamp. Many of
them felt aggrieved by the emancipation of their
Hottentot slaves, and determined to remove to
distant localities, where they could erect themselves into a republic, and pursue without moles-
tation the ' proper treatment of the blacks,' viz.
compulsory unpaid labour. One section of this
class of persons penetrated the interior as far as
the Cashan mountains, whence a Zulu chief, named
Mosilikatze, had been expelled by Dingaan. They
came with the prestige of white men and deli-
verers; but the Bechuana, who had just escaped
the hard sway of the Caffres, soon found ' that
Mosilikatze was cruel to his enemies and kind to
those he conquered, but the Boers destroyed their
enemies and made slaves of their friends.' . . .
I have myself seen Boers come to a village and,

according to their custom, demand twenty or thirty women to weed their gardens. These poor creatures accordingly proceeded to the scene of unrequited toil, carrying their own food on their heads, their children on their backs, and instruments of labour on their shoulders. 'We make the people work for us,' said the Boers, 'in consideration of allowing them to live in our country.' . . . The demand for domestic servants must be met by forays on tribes which have good supplies of cattle. . . . It is difficult to conceive that men . . . should set out after caressing their wives and children, and proceed to shoot down men and women whose affections are as warm as their own. They trace their descent from some of the best men (Huguenots and Dutch) the world ever saw. In their own estimation they are the chosen people of God, and all the coloured race are 'black property' or 'creatures'—heathen given to them for their inheritance. Living in the midst of a much more numerous native population, and at fountains removed many miles from each other, the Boers feel themselves insecure, and when they receive reports against any tribe from some dissatisfied black, the direst vengeance appears to them a simple measure of self-defence. However bloody the massacre, no qualms of conscience ensue. . . . The Bakwains had the spectacle of various tribes enslaved before their eyes. . . . During the period of eight years no winter passed without some of the tribes being plundered of both cattle and children by the Boers. Friendly tribes are forced to accompany a party of mounted Boers, and are ranged in front to form ' a shield.' The Boers then coolly fire over their heads till the devoted people flee and leave cattle, wives, and children to the captors. This was done in nine cases during my residence in the interior, and on no occasion was one drop of Boer blood shed. Letters were repeatedly sent by them to Sechele, ordering him to surrender himself as their vassal. He replied, ' I was made an independent chief and placed here by God and not by you. I was never conquered by Mosilikatze, as those tribes whom you rule over, and the English are my friends.' . . . The Boers, 400 in number, were sent by the late Mr. Pretorius to attack the Bakwains in 1852, and, besides slaughtering a number of adults, carried off 200 of our school-children into slavery. The people under Sechele defended themselves, and having killed a number of the enemy, the first ever slain by Bechuana, I had the credit of having taught them to destroy Boers! My house was plundered in revenge; English gentlemen, who had left stores in the keeping of the natives, were robbed of everything; the books of a good library, my solace in our solitude, were torn to pieces; my stock of medicines was smashed, and all our furniture and clothing were carried off and sold."

SOME ACCOUNT OF THE BOERS OF SOUTH AFRICA.

The Cape of Good Hope was discovered by the Portuguese, 1486; the English followed, 1601–20; the Dutch came in 1652, and in 1658 imported slaves from Angola and Guinea. Hottentots and bushmen were the aborigines, and these were brought into subjection.

In 1686 French Huguenots to the number of 97 families joined the Dutch. They imparted to them their earnest religious feelings. They soon lost their language, but their French names remain; Joubert, Boer leader, is one of these; Beck, Duplessis, Durant, Malan, Marais, Rousseau, and De Villiers are others. Some had been of high rank in France, others were vine-dressers; they

planted vineyards and made wine at the Cape, at
the Paarl, Stellenbosch, and Constantia.

In 1737 George Schmidt, missionary to the Hottentots, arrived. He found these people sunk in
poverty and in a state of servitude, robbed of their
lands and cattle. The slaves, Malays, many of
them were beginning to give trouble. Hottentots
and bushmen, hunted down by commandos, were
compelled to take service; these commandos were
bodies of armed men, who attacked the native
kraals, killing adults and taking the children as
"apprentices." The servitude of the natives was
not like that of the imported slaves. About 1780
the Dutch first came into collision with another
race—the Kafirs. In 1795 the Cape Colony was
seized by the British, and finally conquered in
1806. In 1808 Moravian missions began, and in
1816 Wesleyan, in South Africa.

Up to the year 1828 the position of the Hottentots had been wretched in the extreme. Now,
in 1829, they gained the rights of freedom and rose
rapidly in the social scale. A Kafir war took place
in 1835. Emancipation of the slaves. There were
34,000 slaves in the colony in 1820—Malagasy,
Malays, and half-breeds. In 1833 passed the
Emancipation Bill, and in 1838 all the Cape slaves

were set free. Now the Dutch, dissatisfied with the elevation of the Hottentots, the restoration of ceded territory to the Kafirs, and the emancipation of the slaves, began to leave the colony in large numbers; they left to escape from English law. By the year 1837, 1,000 waggons had arrived in Natal, which had been granted by Dingaan to William IV., through Captain Allen Gardiner, in 1836. Retief and his 70 companions were basely murdered by Dingaan in 1838, in sight of Rev. H. Owen, missionary of the Church Missionary Society in Zululand. This was followed by the invasion of Natal by the Zulus, who put to death some 300 of the Dutch (men, women, and children) in Weemer. The Dutch Boers sided with Panda, divided the nation, and deposed Dingaan. The British took possession of Natal in 1843.

The Rev. W. C. Holden, author of the " History of Natal," says:—

" Early in the year 1840 I arrived in Colesberg (near the Orange river) with my family. The great event of the time was the emigration of the Dutch farmers beyond the Orange river. This self-expatriation arose mostly from their slaves having been taken away from them. . . . In 1841 I went to Platberg and saw for myself how

things were. The Dutch were mere squatters;
everyone seemed to do what was right in his own
eyes."

To have a good gun and know how to use it,
was regarded as one of the great acquisitions of
that time.

" A good waggon constituted the house and
home of many of these wanderers in pastures new,
where they might dwell without being under the
control of the British Government.

" As time rolled on, the Dutch farmers continued
to cross the Orange river. They had no regular
government and were not subject to law, conse-
quently violence and crime increased ; matters
grew worse, until it became necessary for the
British to step in, which was done by Sir Harry
Smith annexing the country to the Cape colony
and establishing a government over it. This was
resented by the farmers. The battle of Boomplaats was fought, in which an easy victory over
them was achieved, and they submitted to British
rule. Major Warder was appointed commissioner.
Magistrates were established, the country being
designated the Orange River Sovereignty. This
mode of government was being worked until
Sir George Cathcart, in an unfortunate moment,

resolved to humble Moshesh, Basuto chief. In attempting to do this he was defeated, and, unhappily, advised her Majesty's Government to abandon the sovereignty. To carry out this Sir G. Clerk was sent out, who, despite the most urgent opposition on the part of the British colonists and many of the Dutch, effected a suicidal transfer of the country from the English to the Dutch. The Orange Free State and the Transvaal republics were formed, and for many years poor and feeble governments were carried on, until the discovery of the Diamond Fields."

The Bishop of Capetown visited the Orange River State in 1850. From his journal I take the following:—

" 1850, *April* 30*th.*—Left Colesberg for Bloemfontein. The first house in the sovereignty belongs to an English farmer. *May* 1*st.*—The country throughout consists of large plains, bounded by low mountains or rocky koppies (little hills). There is abundance of game—the gnu, bless bok, and spring bok. There are also a great many cranes, and some fine eagles. We stayed at Mr. Wright's farm at Boomplaats, and I surveyed the field of Sir Harry Smith's late battle with the Boers. The rebels were posted behind some strong koppies, but retreated speedily from one to the other, until their retreat became a rout. I visited the graves of our brave officers and soldiers, who are buried in a walled enclosure in Mr. Wright's garden. I read our office for the burial of the dead over their remains. In the capital and only village in the sovereignty the population is nearly exclusively English. . . . . 7th.—Started for Thaba Nchu. The Vaal river is now the boundary which separates the sovereignty from the Boers, who refuse to recognise British authority. These men have formed themselves into a Republic (South African), and have their 'Raad' (council). The exact constitution, however, of their government they have not yet fixed, though they have had many meetings. I understand they are about 10,000 in number. Their feelings are very bitter against the English Government. Some regard that Government as Antichrist, some the Queen in person. They took Dr. Frayer, of Bloemfontein, prisoner, for presuming to cross the Vaal River while hunting, having no permission to enter their territory. It appears quite clear, I think, that they have among them a modified form of slavery. . . . There is a party of them who think they are on their way to Jerusalem, and that they are not very

far distant from it. They are deceived by the
apparent nearness of Egypt in the maps of their
old Bibles. There are systems of a growing
fanaticism amongst these poor people. The Dutch
Boer, wherever he may be, under whatever circumstances, never casts off his respect for religion.
There is nothing sceptical in his mind. His religion,
however, is traditionary. It exercises no great
influence over him. He is very superstitious.—
Note 1. The following is from ' The Friend of the
Sovereignty ':—' We are informed that Potgieter
has destroyed the chiefs, but has killed many of the
people, taking captive about 300 of their children,
who are declared to have been sold as slaves to the
Portuguese at Delagoa Bay. Pretorius disapproved
of the conduct of Potgieter. . . . 800 of them
are opposed to any law or government whatever,
and only a few of the latest trekkers have a friendly
feeling towards the English Government, and these
dare not express their views. The total number
capable of bearing arms within the Republic is
3,600.' "—Journal, 1850.

On the 17th January 1852, the British Government recognised the independence of the Transvaal.
The treaty contained nine clauses. The fourth
prohibited slavery. The *Cape Argus* of the 12th

December 1876, remarks:—" Through the whole course of this Republic's existence it has acted in contravention of the Sand River Treaty." (See " History of the Zulu War," by Frances E. Colenso, page 117.) " Slavery has been one of the institutions of the country. It has been at the root of most of its wars." (See article by Lord Blachford in " The Nineteenth Century Review," August 1879, p. 265.) Dr. Livingstone was residing among the Bakuena, under the chief Sechele, when the Boers attacked them and took 1,200 prisoners, mostly children. Dr. Livingstone's house was pillaged and all his property carried away or destroyed. (See his Missionary researches and travels.) In 1853 died Pretorius the great Boer leader.

The Bapedi, under Sekwati and his son Sekukuni, came into collision with the Boers. Potgieter arrived in their country in 1848, and professed to buy the land for 100 head of cattle. (See " History of the Zulu War," p. 114.) The war between the Boers and Bapedi arose out of similar encroachments on the part of the Boers, which led to their border disputes with the Zulus. The Boers gradually deprived the natives of their land thus : They first rented land from the chiefs, then built upon it.

Finally, they professed to have bought the land for the sum already paid as rent, announced themselves the owners of it, and were shortly levying taxes on the very men whom they had dispossessed. In this way Sekukuni was declared by the Boers to have ceded to them hundreds of square miles for 100 head of cattle. In 1876 the Volksraad declared war against Sekukuni. A stronghold was attacked, but the Boers were seized with a panic and fled. The stragglers reached Pretoria, completely demoralised, and their allies, the Amaswazi, enraged at the cowardly conduct of the Boers, threatened to sack the town. From this time the Transvaal Boers were regarded as weak and cowardly. They hired mercenaries under Von Schlickman to carry on the war. For a time the Republic seemed to be at the mercy of the Bapedi. Sekukuni claimed a large tract of country occupied by Boers for thirty years. The Treasury was empty, and the burghers said they could not pay the war-tax. The burden of the public debt pressed heavily upon the people. The peace of all the colonies was imperilled. . . Then came the annexation. (See History of the South African Republic, in the " Compendium of South African History," by G. M'C. Theal Lovedale, 1877.)

Before the annexation a commission (composed of

Captain Clarke, R.A., and Mr. Osborne) was sent
by Sir Theo. Shepstone to inquire into a treaty
pressed by the Boers upon Sekukuni, and rejected
by him. To these gentlemen " Sekukuni stated
that the English were great and he was little
(Blue Book, c. 1776), that he wanted them to
save him from the Boers, who hunted him to and
fro, and shot his people down like wild game. He
had lost 2,000 men by the war, ten brothers, and
four sons. He could not trust the Boers." We
now turn to the other chief pretext for the annexation, viz. the disturbed condition of the Zulu border.
" Ketchwayo himself says I have never given or
sold any land to the Boers of the Transvaal."
(" The Zulu War," p. 150).

One of the officers who fell at Lang's Nek was
Captain J. Ruscombe Poole, R.A. He published
an account of the Zulu nation and the war as taken
down from the lips of the captive Ketchwayo.
This throws great light on the subject of the
Boers.

" Macmillan's Magazine" for February 1880,
had the following:—

" The Boers had now appeared on the field at
Natal. Pieter Retief and his party went to (1838)
Dingaan. The Boers tried to outwit Dingaan.

The end of it was, Retief and his party were murdered. After Retief's death Dingaan invaded Natal, and killed a great many of the Boers. About a year after this (1839), the Boers invaded Zululand, and were defeated. The Zulus again invaded Natal. After this the Boers again invaded Zululand, and built a laager on the Blood River, and then raided from it, harassing the country. Panda fled from Dingaan, and threw in his lot with the Boers. Ketchwayo accompanied his father. The Boers in January 1840, invaded Zululand again with Panda and his army. Dingaan was defeated, and Panda became King, but was obliged to make a treaty with the Boers, by which he gave up Natal. The English, under Smith, came and defeated the Boers. The Dutch then trekked over the Drachensberg, and asked Panda to give them leave to live in the country adjoining Utrecht; this Panda allowed, and the country where Utrecht now stands he gave nominally to a Boer (one of the Landtmans ?) who was to be the outside or border Boer. Panda was very glad to see the English take Natal from the Boers; he did not trust them. The English soon began to increase and occupy the whole of Natal. Trade increased, and blankets were in reach of all. Panda died in October 1872.

Towards the end of his reign the Boers encroached
a good deal, both east and north, building and
settling down on the Zulu side of Utrecht, in the
Luneburg district, where they went for wood.
They were often reminded that they were on Zulu
soil. The Boers at one time endeavoured to buy
the Utrecht district; they sent 200 head of cattle
to Panda for this purpose, but he refused to sell the
land. He accepted 100 head as tribute for the
Boer living at Utrecht. After this the Boers kept
on encroaching, and treated the border Zulus with
much harshness. Panda was averse to war, and
would not press his rights. After Panda's death
the same sort of trouble continued. Then the
Boers had a quarrel with Umbelini; he was a
Swazi, settled in Zululand. When Mr. Shepstone
came to Ketchwayo's coronation, Ketchwayo spoke
to him about the encroachments of the Boers.
Mr. Shepstone said he would make inquiries, and
sent two Natal chiefs and a white man to see and
report on the disputed territory. The white man
told Ketchwayo that the Boers were in the wrong,
and that they would tell Mr. Shepstone so. After
the annexation of the Transvaal, Mr. Shepstone met
the Zulus at Conference Hill to hear the boundary
dispute. Every Zulu chief of any note came. Only

a few Boers were present. Mr. Shepstone said:
' If I were called upon to point out what I consider
to be a fair boundary, I should say the Blood River
and the Old Hunting Road.' The Zulu chiefs
would not agree to this, and went away much
dissatisfied. The nation was very hostile towards
the Boers on account of the frequent frontier
disturbances, and there is no doubt that a very little
fuel to the fire already smouldering would have
brought on a war between the Boers and Zulus.
Ketchwayo himself was against a war, although he
threatened to fight the Boers, but admits that had
not the Transvaal been annexed, it was only a
question of time how soon war would have broken
out between the Boers and Zulus. The Zulus had
no animosity against the English. Ketchwayo
(Cetywayo) asked Mr. Shepstone to place a magistrate on the Transvaal border to settle border
disputes. Ketchwayo was not satisfied with the
decision of the commission on the Transvaal
boundary."

I have now quoted enough for my purpose. As
one who has lived in the country, and whose
offspring have settled there, I may be allowed to
say that, together with my fellow-countrymen in
South Africa, I cannot but regard the present peace

as hollow. In concluding such a peace, the interests
of the British colonists and loyal Boers have been
ignored. Moreover, as far as we can foresee, it
will cause the natives to rise against Boer rule,
besides causing rivalry between the Dutch and the
British. If we ignore right of conquest, and wish
to restore independence to the people, then surely
the natives of the country have the first claim upon
us, and not the Boers, whose right to the Transvaal
is very doubtful indeed ; for we conquered the
natives, not they. To make the best of the present
state of things I would divide the country, assigning
one portion to the Boers, one to the natives under
British protection, and another, viz. the Utrecht
district, to the British. This district is Cisvaal,
not Transvaal.

PART IV.

ZULULAND AFTER THE WAR.

Basuto Occupation of Zululand.—When Zenzangakona (Tshaka's father) was chief of the Zulus
(they being at that time but a small tribe), a Basuto
tribe occupied this district from the head of the
Nquto range of mountains, stretching all down
past Isandhlwana to the Buffalo (Umzinyati) river.
They took in the whole of what was called Sihhayo's
district and a great deal more. Their chief was
Seka. Zenzangakona was succeeded by Tshaka
(Chaka), and Seka, the Basuto, by Wcza. Tshaka
made war with Weza and overcame him. He
could not destroy all his people, but drove them
westward into the country lying between the Free
State and the Transvaal. There they multiplied
fast, and were joined by other Basuto from the

neighbourhood, until they became very powerful. But a civil war broke out, and at the same time they were attacked by Korannas, helped by some Dutch settlers. By this they were broken up and separated into three different portions. Their troubles were many and great. One portion took refuge in Natal under Umbunda, Hlubi's father, and so it happened that Hlubi and his people are simply returning to the homes of the fathers (amanxiwa, a kwabo).

They take a quiet sort of pride in pointing out to me a few piled-up *stones*, plainly denoting that a kraal has been there in ages past, and saying, " Our fathers' homesteads."*

Ketchwayo's challenge (question) to the Dutch of the Transvaal, during the late disputed boundary question, was " Kombani amanxiwa akini," " Point out the old sites of your people." These, as you know, are the great proof in their eyes of the ownership of land.

It seems strange that the Imperial Government, without knowing it, should be the means of bringing these people back to the homes of their fathers.

---

* Ruined *stone* kraals; a proof of old Basuto occupation of Zululand. Zulus do not build stone kraals; Basuto do.

Placing Hlubi here was the best thing done during the settlement of the Zulu chieftain question. Of course I cannot tell whether Sir Garnet Wolseley grasped the likely consequence of placing a man like Hlubi over this district, which is the key to Zululand, but nothing could have been better both for themselves and the people of Natal. The Zulus themselves will be great gainers by Hlubi being placed over them. Their late chief, Usihhayo, was really no chief, but only a man placed in authority by the Zulu king. He was not even a Zulu native. Shortly after the Isandhlwana disaster, he was eaten up by Umnyamana, because so many women had been to the king crying and saying that their children and husbands were all dead, and asking him why he had begun (*qala*) to fight against the whites, asking also that Usihhayo and his people should be eaten up.

So Umnyamana was sent with an impi against them. They killed a great many of the people and took away everything they could get. Now, instead of depriving Usihhayo's people of their lands and homes, we have done everything we could to resettle them. Hlubi takes the place of Usihhayo ; that is the only change. The district is a very large one, so that a few more people among them do not hurt the first inhabitants, especially as when the whole of Hlubi's people have come here they will not make up the number lost during the war. They have lost more than in any part of Zululand. They are really destitute. All their crops, too, have failed this year, and as they have no cattle to buy food with, I do not know what they will do. Hlubi strives hard to make them like him. Since he has been in Zululand he has inquired why Umnyamana took their cattle away, and as he has found out that the cattle were never given up to the King but were kept by Umnyamana, Hlubi, by the authority of the British Resident, is making him disgorge everything he took from Usihhayo's people and return them to their lawful owners.

This has won greatly on the hearts of the people. Hlubi is bringing about 500 of his own people, who are settling down and mixing with the Zulus. They are greatly superior to the Zulus, and are an improving tribe. They have just reached that stage of knowledge when they are able to grasp the full meaning of "education" and the benefits to be derived therefrom. I heard Hlubi telling his council (Ibandhla), composed of the head Zulus of this district assembled at his house, that Zululand

in the late war was "Ignorance" and England
"Knowledge," and that had they listened and
attended to the "teachers" sent to teach them
they would never have had to cry over the graves
of so many of their best men   One of the greatest
obstacles to the advancement of the Zulus is the
debased condition of their *women*.   It was bad
enough in Natal ; it is worse here.   They are,
indeed, *beasts* of *burden*.   Now Hlubi's people, the
Basuto, treat their women in a very different
manner.   In many cases they are more advanced
than the men.   They have none of the outdoor
work to do; the men do that.   They are better
treated than the women of the English peasantry.
Again, although many of them are polygamists,
Hlubi is trying his best to check it, not so much
because he thinks it wrong, but on the principle
that a nation of polygamists can never rise to be
very great.   The Basuto are all eager to learn, and
that all their children should be taught.   Now 500
people, such as I have described, settling down in
a district like this, and mixing with the Zulus on
terms of equality, must have a good effect.   I can
see a change already, in that the kraals all round
are looking about for ploughs, so that their women
may be released from the hard task of tilling the

soil. They are also beginning to pick up pieces of apparel, from seeing the Basuto women coming to service dressed.

That it is a good thing for the people of Natal that Hlubi has been placed here is very plain. He and his people have proved themselves good and loyal subjects of England's Queen, always ready to obey the call of the English chief, no matter what the work may be. They have got such a thorough trust and confidence in the English, and such an admiration of the greatness of the British nation, that their one great wish is to learn to be more like them. They are always talking about England's greatness, and how that greatness is all gained by learning, and how she is always wishing to teach other nations, and what a great advantage it is to the black races in Natal, as it will be here in Zululand, to have the English for friends.

And when we come to think that Hlubi and his people are looked up to and very much respected by *all the native chiefs* of Zululand, one cannot but acknowledge that it would have been hard to have found a better man than Hlubi as head of this important district. He has a good deal of straight-forward common sense that commands the respect of both whites and blacks. He and some of his

men came to meet me as soon as I crossed the
river Buffalo, and soon after we took a rough
survey of his district, and came to the conclusion
that three other schools at least would be necessary
besides the one at Isandhlwana, as he wanted all
his people to learn. He promised to help in putting
up school-buildings, and said that all the people in
the neighbourhood of each school would be very glad
to come to learn. We then took note of the best
sites for the buildings ; and he asked me to do my
best to get the Bishop to send others to help as soon
as possible, for " he wished all his people to become
Christians, and that, although he was still very
ignorant, he had been taught so far by the Church,
and he wished all his people to be taught by the
same." He ended by saying that if the Church had
refused to teach his people, he should have been
glad for others to come and teach them; but until the
Church had told him that she was unable to do so,
he did not think he should be doing right to allow
others to come. I feel more and more every day
what a great and solemn responsibility rests upon
the Church.

Description of Isandhlwana.—I must describe
what Isandhlwana is like. The place chosen for
the house, &c. is a few hundred yards to the left of

Isandhlwana. But the church will be on the very site of the camp of the 24th Regiment. There are now three huts and three tents. One large tent we have for meals ; it is full of stores. We are to turn out of this directly and leave it for a service tent. The other large one is just finished. Now for the huts. One is a regular native hut for all the boys working ; of these there are a large number, besides those always on the spot. Mr. Johnson calls up any number he wishes to do any special work. Hlubi has told them all that they must help, and well they do it, so that often we have quite a little army of Zulus working away. The other two huts are the usual round ones, thatched down to the ground. There is a little kitchen-garden and a cattle-kraal at some distance. At the back of us are hills, which keep us nicely sheltered; in front are beautiful hills, and chief of these is Isandhlwana rock itself, a very remarkable hill. It is not very large, but steep; the top is more like a stone ruin than a natural pile. On one side are rocks piled up near the top, and on this side the ascent is more gradual, but still with grand-looking rocks. There a is flat piece of grass near the top and another on the top. Trees are scattered about all over ; many are grown in amongst the stones, which seem to form a wall as it were. There is a large cave upon it, some day to be explored. The hill stands alone, apart from any other hill, and when the setting sun is behind it, or a thunder-cloud, it looks magnificent. It is but a few hundred yards from our place.

The battle began on the hills behind us. We have found several skeletons, which we have buried. On the place where the numbers fell under the ledge where the camp was, the grass is yards high, and rank beyond what one could believe without seeing it. All traces are effectually concealed by it, unless you look close. Even then you see little in the way of bones, for they are mostly well buried, except a few stray ones. On the side of the tents, the ground is still strewn with nails, screws, and cartridges (from which the Zulus extracted the powder and shot), and any number of tent-pegs, and those little wooden links for holding the ropes. All things of this sort which we require we get from the field. Standing on the battle-field and looking round, one realises, as one never could before, how it all happened on that awful day; and when one sees the distances they skirmished from the camp, one wonders how they could have been so foolish as to wander away and

scatter themselves in that way. The strangest
thing at first is to be living with the very Zulus
that fought there, and to see them as peaceful and
quiet as possible, and coming in numbers to work
and worship, and talking over that fight even with
the Natal natives (two of whom came with us to
drive the waggon), and to see them coming to
Charles as their umfundisi (teacher), and inkosi
(chief). All this seemed very strange at first.
One old man amuses me very much. He was one
of those who fought on that day, and here he is
dressed fully, even to a hat and collar, and coming
every day trying to do all he can. The day after
we came, we were trying to make our hut nice.
Our Mabuka was very anxious to do all he could,
and if he saw me carrying anything, he said, " Why
do you not tell me to take that ? Give me a great
deal to do. What chief is afraid of his people who
want to work hard for him? " Then he would
seize on things and try to put them tidy, and
anticipate anything I wanted by watching hard.
I have seen little of the Basuto yet ; they are
busy getting their houses built, and their things
from Estcourt. Hlubi came one day; he is a fine-
looking man. A few others have been at different
times.

Visit of the Ex-Empress of France.—To-morrow we expect the Empress may pay us a visit. She is now within a mile or so from this. General Wood, who is with her, passed through this place yesterday, attended by some Basuto. They asked for some milk, and Charles sent two of our boys down to their camp with some. The boys returned, saying they had been set down to eat meat with knives and forks, and they ate and ate till they could eat no longer. The Empress sent up an officer to thank Charles in her name, and that of her suite, for the milk, &c. He brought the Duc de Bassano's compliments, and said the Empress hoped to call the next day. Charles sent her some opera-glasses, found on the field; for we heard that they found hardly anything. In return he received a letter from Sir Evelyn Wood, thanking him in her name.

There was a large congregation to-day, the largest we have ever had. Oh! when you can, please collect for us any amount of clothes for the natives. Any sort of clothes, any size, shape, or colour ; we are not in the least particular up here in the wilds. We shall want a great many when we get all three places going. The natives here, having never had anything of the sort before, wear anything. The clothing ought to be made of good strong stuff.

Dearth and Famine.—Thank you for the medicine you say you have sent out; I can't tell you how acceptable your box will be, for it will enable me to do so much more for these poor people; I use the word poor advisedly. There is great scarcity of food around us now. In fact it is a famine. Many of the people have literally nothing to eat but roots or boiled stalks of maize. The troops destroyed all the food. If it is bad now, what will it be before the next year's crops, especially if the season is late. This year the crops are nothing, for they were sown too late? Maize is £2 a sack, and hard to get.

June 20th, 1880.—As they have no cattle to buy food with, I really don't know what they will do. I do what little I can. Indeed, I have done for them more than I ought ; I have gone beyond my means. The whole neighbourhood comes for food. I have been keeping four kraals for more than a month past, and as they have really nothing wherewith to buy clothing, you can quite understand how very acceptable any covering will be to half-starved children, to say nothing of the older people.

I have got thirteen boys working for me. They are all bound to me, with their own and with their father's consent, for two or five years. They will in time, I hope, become Christians. Give our thanks to those who are sending us clothing, &c.

We have made a good many additions to our establishment since I last wrote. There are three new huts nearly finished. One is a very large one, and is to be used for divine service, and for a schoolroom. It is some distance from the rest, towards the hill. The others are of ordinary size : one is for Mr. Samuelson, son of the missionary, whom we may expect soon, and the other is for visitors. We have moved the harmonium into the dining-tent for service, which we have in English every morning and evening, and on Sunday evening. The native service is in the afternoon.

Mr. Ransom's things have just come, and with them a bell which Mr. Alington brought out. Mr. Ransom has just come from Utrecht, bringing the bell with him. It has been set up outside the large new hut. There is a nice spring of water a little way off, and the water has been brought to our doors.

The natives bring us a great number of things found on the battle-field ; they must have an immense quantity hidden away. They tell us that if it had not been for the plunder on the field, the whole army would have come on after the fight; but their leaders could not get them on. They say it is clever strategy on our part to take so many things about with the army to engage the enemy's attention. A man brought a pair of opera-glasses yesterday ; a variety of things is brought. The commonest are pickaxes ; they have brought so many of these, that we laugh and say we shall take a contract for a road through Zululand.

August 12th, 1880.—We are having a stone building put up for a school chapel. The church on the site of the camp will not be begun for some time to come. Our present church-hut is wonderfully nice.

You will have heard of the appointment of Archdeacon McKenzie as Bishop of Zululand. It seems a long time to wait for him to come out. He will hardly be here before Christmas. Well! when he does come, may he make a thorough good missionary bishop.

Charles is now reading three or four hours a day with Mr. Ransom, and Charles is giving him in return (with Mr. Paton and Mr. May) lessons in Zulu.

Last Sunday I began to take our boys for a short Sunday-school. I am to give them an hour every

Sunday morning. Last Sunday I had only time to explain a picture to them. I was astonished to find how much they remembered of what they had heard in church, evidently showing that they paid great attention. One of them some time ago said he should like to become a Christian. He went to ask his father's consent, and obtained it.

Many of them are getting on very well with their reading and writing at the evening school. We have just had a new little hut put up for a vestry close to the church.

It has been cold the last few days. We see the snow lying on the tops of the hills not far off. It has been actually snowing here.

We have just got three waggon-loads of poles and wattles to Hlubi's own place, to make a beginning there. He is extremely anxious for this, as only the men can come here to service. It is about twelve miles off. There is to be a church-hut, and another put up at once, and then Charles will ride over every alternate Sunday and give them services. They have eleven children there ready to be baptised.

There is another place at which Charles is anxious to make a commencement as soon as possible. This is at Susa's. He is a petty chief in this district, and Hlubi has allowed a good many of the Edendale native Christians to come and settle at his place. He lives about twelve miles away. He it was that turned out his men (fifty in number) to cut poles, &c., and carry them here to build huts for us to live in.

The House at Rorke's Drift.—Mr. Krapt is busy building a house, &c. for the restoration of the mission at Rorke's Drift, under the far-sighted Otto Witt, who has come back with grand plans and ideas.

We are having two sitting-room huts put up now. One is a little one just for Charles and myself, almost touching our hut, which is at present both bed-room and sitting-room. The other is on the site of the large old tent, which has been taken down as it is wanted at Hlubi's for Mr. Norris and some of the boys, who are going to put up the huts. This is for everyone, and is very large indeed. Both are to have *chimneys*—is not that grand? They are to be made of bricks, which have just been manufactured for the purpose. The chimney of the big hut is already built; it looks very peculiar standing by itself. We are beginning to get the breaking-up weather which comes before summer. We had a heavy fall of rain the other evening, and our huts are not waterproof. Our hut was like a sieve ; there was hardly a dry spot. We had to tie up an umbrella to the head of the bed, which looked ridiculous.

On Saturday we went over to bury bones on Isandhlwana, taking boys with us to dig a pit, into which bones could be thrown from time to time. There are many bones still lying about, and even those which are supposed to be buried are only half-hidden. Charles has promised to bury all that may be left now, to save more burying-parties coming. A gentleman who had a brother killed here, has been staying with us. He does not seem in the least affected by coming to the spot where his brother met his sad fate.

We are now enjoying potatoes, peas, cabbages, and lettuces from our garden, which is flourishing in consequence of being regularly watered every morning, which our delightful supply of water allows us to have done. Another garden is being made out of another old cattle-kraal a short way off. These old cattle-kraals come in very useful. When the walls have been repaired, there is a fence all ready for use, which is very necessary with so many cattle about. We hear our new

Bishop intends bringing out a large party, and coming straight to Isandhlwana.

September 13*th*, 1880.—Your letter enclosing £20 came this morning. Thank you so very much for it. It will, indeed, be useful. Just after it came Charles had to start off to Hlubi's to set a little boy's arm, very badly broken by a kick from a horse.

By the same post came the news that our case had been despatched to Maritzburg. Fancy only hearing now! I hope we may be able to get it ere long. Poor Archdeacon Fearne has had his house burnt down, being able to save nothing. Alderley was blown down, and the Trevors left homeless on the very same day. They had a narrow escape. On Sunday morning Charles went to take a service at a place a short distance off, where Hlubi has allowed a great many of the Edendale Christians to come and settle. It is about an hour's ride from this, so Charles was back in time to take the native service here. He had such a nice service. He sent word the day before that he was coming ; so they had prepared to receive him. They had put up a large awning, under which were a table and chair for him, and ranged in a great pile on the opposite side of the table were a large number of Bibles and Prayer Books in a variety of dialects, chiefly Xosa (Kafir), as they used that version first. They gave Charles a prayer-book to use, which they said was Wesleyan. There seemed hardly any difference between it and ours. There was a large and attentive congregation. They were all nicely dressed (*i.e.* the Edendale people), the women and children in clean print dresses. After service they regaled him with tea and bread. He says the bread was excellent, made by one of the women. They sang very well; one girl took the lead. They are very anxious to have someone settled at their place to teach them. They promise to build him his house and school-room.

Hearing these accounts of outlying places will give you an idea of the immense amount of work in this district, and Charles alone to do it. There was a very good congregation here, too, on Sunday afternoon. Our little church was closely packed. They are beginning to sing quite nicely now (at least our own boys are) the hymns they have been taught to sing in the evening. They still understand but imperfectly when they ought to come in. Last Sunday they all took to repeating the prayers in a low voice after Charles. My Sunday-school class is very nice ; for besides these boys, others come in and learn, four or five women and girls, and an occasional man or two. They are very attentive and remember fairly what they have been told, on being questioned. They appreciate pictures now. You know at first they are utterly meaningless to them. They look at them without a notion that they are intended to represent anything, and it takes some time before their eyes become sufficiently educated up to them to understand them. I always found this at Springvale, even with fresh children.

November 9th, 1880.—A most curious incident happened the other day.

An elderly native living near the Blood river, who has a widespread fame as an "Umtakati" (wizard), and who, as a rain doctor, has gotten to himself herds of cattle and fifteen wives, wishes to turn over a new leaf and become a Christian. His plan is to put away all his wives but one, build them huts, and let them go and live as "Onina wabat-wana" (mothers of children). He will divide his wealth among these, and then go and live with one wife after he has been baptised. I was surprised. He was a very noted character in Zululand in Ketchwayo's time. I shall have more to write about this man. You will understand the state of excitement we were in when our box arrived. We shall never be able to thank you enough for it.   It came opportunely.   As Margaret has just begun her Day and Sunday School, a great many children of both sexes have come.   The poor little things come as naked as they were born.   You should have seen their delight when they were clothed.   To be thus taken care of is such a new and unheard-of idea to them, that they hardly know what to make of it.   Children in Zululand are very little cared for.   I wonder if those kind hearts that set industrious fingers to work making clothing for these little naked people, ever realise the joy they give.   Those working parties have far more to do with mission-work among the heathen than is ever dreamt of.   What few tools I had I had sent over to the builders, so you can understand with what joy I pounced upon Graham's box of nails, gimlets, &c. The medicines are very well chosen indeed. Margaret's children looked very well at service— twenty-nine cleanly-dressed children—the envy of the neighbourhood.   The famine is raging worse and worse.   Since the waggon came from Maritz- burg with maize, there has been a crowd of natives begging.   I have already spent more than my year's stipend in buying maize.

Everyone has been for a hunt to-day, whites

and blacks. They started soon after 5 A.M. and
came back this afternoon, having killed only four
bucks and no birds. Charles shot three out of the
four. They went to get game for Christmas Day,
when there will be so many people here.

On New Year's Day a tall, very dark clergy-
man appeared on horseback. Everyone thought it
was the Bishop, but Mr. Ransom came up and
recognised him as a friend of his, a Mr. Swinny,
whom he had last seen in Capetown, as chaplain to
the Bishop. Mr. Swinny explained that our Bishop
would be here that day week, and that he himself
belonged to his party, having volunteered for the
work as the Bishop passed through Capetown.
Sure enough, on that day week two riders were
discerned coming from an unusual quarter. We
exclaimed " There is our Bishop ! " and rushed to
meet him. Mr. Shildrick was with him, having
come as his guide. He was tired and travel-
stained, but the more we saw of him the more we
liked him. He seems just the man for the work.
He is tall and dark, and not much over forty. He
stayed from Saturday till Tuesday. He is going
to fetch up all his party to St. Andrew's at once,
because there is a good house there, and then he
will come to Isandhlwana. This is just what we

have been hoping he would do. Ever since we found that the Basuto were not going to live here we have hoped that we should be settled at Hlubi's own place. Charles will now be able to give his attention to the one place now the Bishop has come. I think it is so splendid how Charles has managed to keep this district for the Church, and to establish all these centres, in spite of many difficulties, and is now able to hand over to the Bishop such a good beginning, and to think he has done it all and got over the first hard work.

The Bishop's first visit to Hlubi.—On Sunday the Bishop rode over to Hlubi's with Charles and Mr. Ransom. His coming had been long and eagerly looked forward to. A large number of people was assembled. The Bishop baptised twenty children, all of them, either scholars of Charles's when he was at Estcourt, Natal (Hlubi's old place), or else their brothers and sisters. They had been ready for some time, but Charles thought it would be nice for the Bishop to find so many little ones ready to be received into the Church. Indeed, the Bishop was exceedingly pleased. At tea-time, when he was back again, he said, " Oh! it was wonderful." It was a marvellous thing to see the Chief and his headmen, and so many of his tribe and people, all gathered together to present their little ones to Christ. Two of the children were Hlubi's own. On Monday, Charles wished to take the Bishop over to the little settlement of Christians at Hlanhlakazi, but they had not time to go.

On Tuesday the Bishop left with Mr. Shildrick; Charles and Mr. Swinny seeing them on their way, and coming home in the evening. You remember Mr. Shildrick coming to Springvale to be ordained by Bishop Callaway, and what a hero he made of John Dunn. I was amused to hear him still stand up for him as warmly as ever.

On Monday last Mr. Ransom left us for England. He hopes to come out again.

The Boers in the Transvaal.—You will have heard of the rising of the Boers in the Transvaal. They have been alarming the people here a great deal. First they began by trying to buy horses from the Basuto, coming by twos and threes; then they threatened to come and take all their horses, and went on to order Hlubi to quit that part of his territory which they claimed as their own. They first asked the Basuto if they were on their side, or on that of the English; and when they said the English, they said they would come and turn them out. Hlubi has had most of the men of his district at his kraal, to be ready if any Boers did come. Numbers of men have been here on their way to and from his kraal, armed with such assegais, &c. as they could get; and Hlubi has been continually sending over messengers to tell Charles of some new threat, and to ask his advice, or for letters to take on to the British Resident to acquaint him with the doings of the Boers. Hlubi said, if he could only get some ammunition and more guns, he would not care for the Boers if they did come; and he got permission from the Resident to force them to leave if they came and made themselves obnoxious, or to take them prisoners.

A party of Boers came into the country and went round to the kraals, trying to make the Zulus rise, promising to bring back Ketchwayo if they would join them. They could not make much impression on them; their hands are too full with their war against the English for them to do much mischief here, however they may threaten. Yet they may raise a spirit of discontent, if they are allowed to go round talking nonsense to the Zulus. So Charles, thinking it right that the Government should be informed, wrote a letter for Hlubi. The answer returned was to the effect that Mr. Osborne had been written to on the subject, that he knew

Hlubi's loyalty, and would not suffer him or his people to be molested, and then ending, rather grandly, by saying that there were large bodies of troops coming, and that the rebellion would soon be quelled. The women and children over at Hlubi's got so much alarmed, that they would not sleep at home, but went up into the rocks and caves for the night.

We* steamed into the Bay of Funchal, and dropped anchor soon after 7 this morning. After breakfast I went ashore, coming back about 4 P.M., after a pleasant day. The island is very beautiful, but the town of Funchal is very comical; all the streets are steep and narrow, paved with small black stones set close together. The houses are flush with the street, without any footpath; they are all white or yellow, shaded by shutters or venetian blinds. The bazaars could not boast of any windows; you enter through wide doors, and the goods are displayed round the room. Over the doors are odd signs, some in French or Portuguese, and some in English. The streets were guarded by slouching-looking police, half-soldiers, who march about in companies of twenty strong. In the middle of the town is the

---

* From my son's letters, on his going out again.—T. B. J.

cathedral, an ugly, white-washed building, with a
curious tower. The chief place of resort is a sort
of central promenade entirely shaded by trees ; in
the centre was a stand for the band. It was summer
weather, the flowers were lovely and in full bloom.
Many of these I had never seen before, such as a
creeper of magenta-coloured flower covering the
walls and trellis-work with a mass of bloom;
another of orange colour was very brilliant. I saw
the eucalyptus, peach, loquat, and some beautiful
palms, and other tropical plants. This part of the
island is rather bare of trees. It is the wet season
here, and everything is fresh and green, except the
vines and other deciduous trees. On the hills are
tanks for irrigation during drought. The mountain torrents are now full, their channels lie through
picturesque gorges. The rocks are of volcanic
origin, very dark. I went up a hill at the back of
the town, from which there was a splendid view,
both on to the mountains and over the bay to the
open sea. Six large steamers lay at anchor in the
bay, and many sailing-ships. There seem to be no
carts or carriages on the island. People go about
in the queerest little ox-sledges, which consist of a
car containing two seats, covered with an awning
and curtains. This is slung on to two sledge-

runners by springs, a pole is fastened in front, and
the whole is drawn along at a smart pace by two
little oxen. Goods are conveyed on a thick plank
or beam of hard wood, turned up before like the
sole of a shoe. Cultivation is on the garden plan.
Fruit is the principal thing grown. The vines are
trained over trellis-work, but the principal vineyards are not in this part of the island. Sugar-cane
is grown in patches. They begin to cut the cane
in February.

The day after leaving Madeira we visited " The
Canaries." We did not pass between Teneriffe
and Gomera, as we did in the " Conway Castle,"
but between Gomera and Palma, which took us
further from the peak, but gave us a good view.
We sighted Cape de Verde on the 2nd, and arrived
safe at Capetown. Everything was parched and
dried up at Capetown. The mountain had no sign
of green upon it.

Feb. 18*th*, 1881.—Came into Algoa Bay on Thursday, and to-day we reached East London. After
leaving we coasted along very near the shore, which
looked fresh and green after the burnt-up appearance of Capetown. The coast consisted chiefly of
low hills covered with grass and bush, with here
and there a ridge of rock running out into the sea.

We arrived off the bluff at Port Natal early on Saturday morning, and went straight over the bar as we did in 1873. Came on to Maritzburg, and called on the Bishop. This place is full of troops. Took postcart for Greytown, forty-five miles. I could get no horse, and so pushed on afoot; got a lift in a waggon, and then on to Mooi River, 20 miles. The country is like the valley of the Umkomazi. Met two natives who had escaped from waggons looted by the Boers, near Newcastle. They burned such waggons as they did not want, and took the rest with all the oxen, pitching away the loads. They let the white men who were with them go free. They described the Boers as being in great numbers from boys to old men, as having plenty of horses, but as short of provisions, and living on meat. At Mooi river I saw two white men, also escaped, who confirmed this.

I left Mooi river and walked to the Tugela. The country is very fine. I rested at the river till sundown, and then started again and reached Umsinga before 10 P.M., twenty-seven miles. Left Umsinga at nine next day, and went as far as Helpmakaar, thirteen miles. The rain was heavy, and so I stayed the night. Left at 7 A.M. next day, and walked to Rorke's Drift, where I was kindly

entertained by Mr. Otto Witt. Here is a queer
part of my story. By taking a short cut, I missed
Margaret (my sister) and Charles, who were on
their way to Umsinga in a waggon. On reaching
the drift, I heard they had passed. I had seen the
waggon without knowing it. Failing to get a horse
to overtake them, I went up to Mr. May's store.
I found May and Paton settled in two tents.
Mr. May knew me at once. I stayed the night
there. Next day to Hlubi's, two miles on, where
new huts are being built of stone. I borrowed a
horse and rode over to Isandhlwana. I found there
Mr. Swinny; he is getting on wonderfully with the
language. I explored the battle-field, which still
retains many traces of that fatal day. There are
three cairns of loose stones erected besides the iron
cross and private monuments. The ground is
strewn with cartridge-cases, bits of tent, chips of
waggons, and pieces of iron.

On Monday I took the one horse, which Charles
had left here, and set off in pursuit, and arrived at
the Gordon Memorial Mission the same evening.
News of the battle of Amajuba, an awful affair.
The head of this mission is Dr. Dalzell, a good
doctor of medicine. Margaret has come hither to
be under him. I arrived here on Monday (yester-

day), and found (my sister) Margaret in front of the house. Charles was out, and I introduced myself to Margaret on the verandah. She was not expecting me, and took me for a stranger. She said I had changed a great deal.

Graham has arrived safe and sound, and looking very well, but so much altered that I did not know him in the least. On Monday Charles had gone to the post, hoping to find a letter from Graham. I was, meantime, surprised by a young man walking into the verandah, where I was lying down reading and enjoying figs and peaches. I got up and made him a polite bow, expecting him to say who he was. To my surprise he came right up and said "Margaret," and then I knew it must be Graham; but it was a long time before I really knew him again, though he produced his credentials. His outward appearance and voice has quite changed. Yet Charles knew him instantly.

Mr. Stewart, of this mission (Free Church of Scotland), has been going about in Zululand for some time, with a spring-cart and a tent, teaching. He came to Isandhlwana on his way out, and hearing that we wanted a carriage, kindly offered us the use of his cart. About half-way to the drift the axle-tree broke. Mr. Stewart was much distressed that we should have broken down; he is such a good fellow. Under his care, and with one wheel locked, the cart went on to the drift with me in it. The blacksmith of the drift could do nothing, so they lifted the cart (with its wheels off) bodily on to the waggon, and secured it there, and so we came on safely to Umsinga.

I have been absent four weeks with the waggon. The Tugela river was so full that we had to go round by Newcastle. We came up with eight waggons belonging to Hlubi and his Basuto, and we kept company with them as far as Estcourt. Whilst they were with us we had to double span a great many times. I give a few specimen days.

March 23rd.—About noon, by the efforts of two spans of picked oxen, both the waggons were got out. We inspanned about 2 P.M. and trekked till 5, making detours to avoid bogs and marshes which were across the road. One waggon stuck fast, but was hauled out in a minute or two.

March 30th.—After waiting a whole day at Lady-smith we found Klip river full and a number of waggons waiting to cross. One waggon made the attempt with four span of oxen (fifty-six), but they were forced to swim, and were carried down by the stream and nearly drowned. Ladysmith is a pretty little town, but lying low, close to the river. There is a camp here of the 58th Regiment, which suffered so heavily at Amajuba mount.

31*st.*—It took the whole day to cross the river. There was the greatest excitement at the drift. An immense number of waggons were waiting on the other side to cross. Every other waggon stuck fast on coming down to the brink, when the yelling and cracking were tremendous. Now and then a waggon from our side forced its way. Two waggons stuck fast hopelessly, and one was smashed to pieces by collision and stopped the way for some time. To add to the confusion, there were spans of oxen continually crossing and recrossing, and a drove of eighty horses had to be swum across and two herds of cattle. Some goats also made the attempt, but gave it up. I wonder they do not make a bridge here. Over the Tugela there is a grand bridge. Whilst we were waiting, several ambulance waggons came down from the front with wounded soldiers. Many of them were on foot with their arms in slings. There are hospital tents at convenient distances along the road, where the ambulances stay the night. I talked with some of the soldiers; one of them gave me an account of that terrible affair at Amajuba mount. He was at the top of the hill with three companies of the 58th, which suffered most. He said that the Boer loss was much under-rated. He said that if the Boers had been disciplined they might have killed or taken prisoners all the force on the hill, but they stopped to plunder, and so those got down who did escape.

April 6*th.*—Met a detachment of the 97th Highlanders marching to the front. Crossed Mooi river by the bridge. Met a detachment of Hussars from India on their way to the front. Conversed with one of the officers, who said they had lost many horses, which were Australian, and that they had now come from one of the nicest stations in India. It took us twenty days to reach Maritzburg. Three weeks going down and only six days coming back.

May 1*st.*—I write to tell you of our safe arrival at our new home, and of the christening of the baby which took place to-day.

I returned from Maritzburg on Easter-day. I will try to describe our new home at Hlubi's place. It is on the side of a hill which slopes very gently below the house and rises behind it very steep and rocky. There is a large flat space where the house stands, and the soil is good all round. A little stream rises higher up, and has been brought right through the place. The view is splendid. In front we look right over a gently sloping plain to the Blood river, with ranges of hills beyond it. Further on to the left is the Buffalo river, Um-zinyati, with the remarkable hill by Rorke's Drift, and the two gum-trees (eucalyptus), which form the most conspicuous mark of the old fort. Hlubi's own place is to the right of us, less than a mile distant, and divided from us by a ridge which runs out from the hill behind. The buildings consist of one large round stone hut, and a large square one built of reeds and plastered inside and out, with an iron roof. It is used as a kitchen and dining-room. There is also another still larger stone hut, not quite finished. They are built of two kinds of stone, a sort of blue granite, which is in awkward round boulders, red outside (iron stained), and a soft coarse-grained grey sandstone, both very abundant close to, the whole hill at the back being piled with them, the sandstone in huge masses, and the granite in boulders. There is also a good stone hut well away at the back for the native boys.

The country is bare and treeless, with nothing near the house but a few castor-oil trees. The only planted trees are fifty young peaches and apricots, doing very well.

Baby was baptised under a gum-tree at Hlubi's house. In the shade was placed a table with a white cloth on it and a basin. The chief stood at the foot of the tree, and a ring of people all stood round and looked on with great interest, men on one side and women on the other. The baptismal service was partly in Zulu and partly Sesutu. Afterwards we were all invited into Hlubi's house.

May 18*th.*—I like the life here very well, and have no lack of work of all sorts. I like this place better than the old station at Isandhlwana. The stone huts are far better. We are erecting a large tent for a school-church. It is put up over a wooden frame. It is a canvas house. Bricks are being made for a small house ; this is troublesome work. The garden is an old cattle-kraal. Sand and stones are being hauled on a sledge. Doors and windows for huts, shelves, tables, &c. have all to be made. All this is in addition to ordinary duties, such as buying maize, killing beef, &c. Charles has a dozen boys working for him, most of them are engaged for a term of years.

May 24*th.*—Describes the same place and events more in detail, *e.g.* the sermon was interpreted into the language of the Basuto, *viz.* Sesutu.

May 31*st*.—About the Boer peace. We live within six miles of the Transvaal border, and see the hills of Utrecht every day. I am very sorry that we gave back the country to the Boers, and *disgusted* that we should do so *after being beaten.* If it *was right* to give them back the *Transvaal*, it ought to have been done before we had thrown away the blood of so many brave men. If it was *not right*, we are in the ignominious position of having done this for fear of being beaten. The Zulus and Basuto here do not regard us as having been vanquished, for that, in their eyes, would involve the whole army *driven back* and Natal overrun and pillaged, whereas they see the troops even further advanced. They think that both sides are tired of the war and wish to come to an agreement. The Transvaal natives, however, say that if the English give up the country they will fight for it themselves. Some of them have already taken up arms against the Dutch. The Boers are getting insolent. They even demand this part of Zululand. Before I came Hlubi called up and armed his men, both Basuto and Zulus, and patrolled the river for several days, as a report had come that the Boers were coming to seize their horses. Several Zulu tribes came to the British

Resident and asked leave to make a raid across the
Blood river to seize the Boer's cattle.

I like the Basuto; they are very civil.
Hlubi makes a first-rate chief, and is anxious to
improve his people. He is trying to check
polygamy. A man living with one wife and in a
proper house is exempt from the hut-tax of 14s.

Our average congregation is sixty, most of
them Basuto men.

The ferry-boat from Rorke's Drift has been
brought here for repairs before it is launched at a
new drift (ford) higher up. We shall soon have
also a "Silo" (barn) stone cistern for storing
maize.

Anecdote.—The other day I went down to
Rorke's Drift to fetch up some poles and beams. A
boy went with me. A sledge with oxen was to
follow. On reaching the river I undressed in order
to swim across. I then found that Tshwapana could
not swim, so I sent him round by the drift, where
he could wade across. I made a bundle of my
clothes and gave them to the lad to take across. I
then plunged in and swam across the river,
scrambling into an old punt on the other side, and
sat there waiting for my clothes. After waiting
nearly an hour, I began to grow impatient and to

find myself in an awkward fix, and to think that I might have to lie concealed till night and then creep under cover of darkness to the store, rather a chilly proceeding on a frosty night: Just then the sledge and oxen appeared on the other bank with three boys. I made signs to them to follow my example and swim across, leaving a small boy with the oxen. This they did, being good swimmers. I then sent one of them to look for Tshwapana and my clothes. They found him calmly seated on the other side, afraid to come across. He succeeded in bringing him over, when I hailed my clothes with delight. Having put them on, I secured the timber from the fort, punted it across, and so into the sledge and home.

Another day I went over to Isandhlwana to see about the harvesting of some maize which Charles had left there, to count some sheep and goats, and to dig up some potatoes. I took my gun with me for the first time since I came up here. I started long before daybreak, and struck across the country. I saw only two bucks too far off. The sun rose just after I got over the Bashee river and reached the foot of the great red cliffs, where the first battle was fought with Sihhayo's men after the invasion of Zululand.

I had hoped to come across some guinea-fowl, which are very plentiful in such valleys as that of the Bashee, but they are generally seen in large flocks of a hundred or so. I stayed the night at St. Vincent's, Isandhlwana. The party there consists of Mr. Swinny, Mr. Colborn, and Miss Barton, and two Germans and a Swede, who have gone there to build the house and memorial church.

It seemed so queer when I was there to see old familiar objects such as the *basin*, in which I washed my hands, which used to be in your dressing-room at Springvale (bought at Mottram 1856, T. B. J.), and which I can remember far back. Even the bell on the table was the little bronze one (1856) we had at Parkstone, Poole. They have left such things to help on the new people who are settling there.

June 3rd.—It has been very cold with high south wind, like an English east wind. Fowls do well, and would multiply fast but for the wild cats. As many as seventeen chickens were taken in one night. We poisoned a large wild cat with a nicely marked skin and claws like a young tiger. An eagle was attracted by its body, which I shot. It was a fine bird with immense stretch from tip to tip.

April 11*th*.—*Zulu Famine Fund*.—It was with sincere gratitude that I received the news that you had started a subscription for me.   I could not do very much when thousands were in want of food, but I did manage to give some maize to everyone who came asking for food.

When maize failed I killed cattle and gave them meat.   I never turned away one person who came crying " hunger." Not reckoning transport (which is very heavy, T. B. J.), it cost me about £45, not reckoning the cost of the native boys and girls apprenticed to me for periods varying from three to five years (of whom I have now got twenty-four), although the *famine added to the expense of their keep.*

I am glad to say that the famine is a thing of the past now.   Not many adults died of starvation. The Zulus are very good herbalists, and can keep off actual starvation for a long time with roots and bulbs, grasses and herbs ; but from living thus so long they suffered from disease.   Only those living among them could see the damage this famine has done.   The Zulus will never forget it.   They will date events from it.

June 16*th*.—We went to visit the grave of the Prince Imperial, or rather his monument erected

on the spot where he was killed, about twenty-five
miles off. We arrived at sunset. We off-saddled
and went to examine the cross. It is much hidden,
being at the bottom of a shallow donga. There is
a small enclosure of rough stone, in the centre of
which is a white stone cross on a low pedestal,
bearing an English inscription simply recording
his death on that spot, and saying that it was placed
there by Queen Victoria. In front is a heap of
stones; a few trees are planted in the enclosure,
some of which are doing well, including some roses
and ivy. At the other end are the graves of the
two troopers who fell with the Prince. It was
quite dark when we left to go home ; we stumbled
on a kraal and got a man to show us the waggon-
road. We reached home at ten minutes past one
A.M. The next day I developed the measles.
On Saturday two officers of the 7th Hussars
arrived from Newcastle. They stayed over Sunday,
and after visiting the battle-field and the Prince's
grave, came back here for Tuesday night.

July 26*th.*—Mr. Arthur Shepstone came from
Hlubi's. After breakfast we went with him to the
battle-field in order to identify the grave of his
brother George, who fell there. Our party consisted of Charles and Mr. S. Hlubi, myself and

Solomon, who was at the battle. While we were approaching Hlubi gave us graphic descriptions of the great battle, pointing out where the Basuto were engaged. After a little search we found the grave. After this we rode over the field; the grass had just been burnt off, leaving the ground bare; many bones have become exposed again by the rains. I found, by way of relic, a pair of scissors. We off-saddled at St. Vincent's, and Miss Barton gave us afternoon tea. We reached home at sunset. The school is getting on; a great number of boys and girls and a few young men attend. The Chief comes himself sometimes, and his wife regularly. He can read and write his own tongue, but is anxious to learn English. He writes from dictation. Several of his people are at the same lesson. We have also a night school. I teach in the evening.

Hlubi is giving £50 towards the church. There have been forty-five baptisms here this year.

August 1881.—The Bishop has turned up at last, three weeks late. He has been visiting all the stations in Zululand and Swaziland as far as the Bomba mountains, thence to Delagoa Bay on foot. He has been absent six weeks, and has travelled 700 miles on horseback.

On Sunday a large congregation assembled.
There were fifteen baptisms, five adults, including
the Chief's wife. She is a very nice woman,
refined and lady-like. Four men and two women
were confirmed.

August 13*th.*—Hlubi called a big hunt in
honour of two officers. We first went to the top
of a rocky hill, Sihhayo's stronghold. The Zulu
beaters were in the valley. I had only one chance
shot and missed. The beaters, 200 in number,
saluted their Chief in the usual warlike manner,
dancing and charging at him and then stopping
and beating their shields. Twelve bucks and two
or three hares were killed. I rode home with
Hlubi and his men, racing on our way home. I
was more lucky the day before yesterday, when I
killed ten of those large rock-pigeons with one
shot.

28*th.*—We have had a snow-storm here, with
cold high winds and showers of sleet. I was out
on horseback all day looking for cattle which had
run before the storm.

August–September.—St. Augustine's, Isandhlwana.
—Almost all the Basuto are anxious to learn.
Some of the boys come to school on horseback, as
they live so far away. Many of those who live too

far off have sent their children here ; many more would do the same if we could take them in.

Sesuto, the language of the Basuto is quite distinct from the Zulu, although the construction is similar, and many words are alike. The French were the first to reduce Ṣesuto to writing, so that it is spelt in the French fashion, which makes the difference between the two languages appear greater.

We have had a good many visitors lately, chiefly officers coming to see Rorke's Drift and the battle-field.

I went to a sale at De Waar store (Dill's) the other day. The buyers were almost all *Boers,* who are the principal inhabitants of the Biggarsberg, about fifteen miles off.

When Sir E. Wood had done with the Transvaal he came into Zululand, and held a meeting of chiefs at Ihlazatshe (the British Resident's place, fifteen miles hence). All came except *Oham,* who knocked up on the road. The old fellow is in such a state from fat and fuddling, that when his people succeeded in getting him fairly mounted on a horse they had to halt every few miles for him to get off and have a sleep.

Hlubi went with a large following of mounted

men.   The meeting took place on the Monday and
Tuesday following the snowstorm.   White magistrates are to be appointed and a hut-tax levied of
10s. a hut.

A few suggestions were submitted to the chiefs,
who retired and consulted.   On their return they
agreed to most of the clauses, but rejected some,
such as forbidding *spirits* in their districts.   Oham
is terribly fond of gin.   They refused to support
a staff of border police.

October 5th.—This part of Zululand is in a very
unsettled state.   There has been fighting in Oham's
district (to the north).

October 9th.—The people around Mr. Weber's
were all coming together that day and arming
themselves to go to fight against Oham.   Parties of
men kept passing whilst I was there, in war-dress
with shields and assagais.   The place of meeting
was a kraal within sight.

I proceeded on my journey, went over a very
steep hill at the back of the station, and descended
into a valley or plain, on the opposite side of
which was the conspicuous and famous hill of
Hlobane.   It is long and flat-topped, very square
and smooth in its general outline, but rugged
enough in detail, as our men found to their cost

during the battle.* We also saw at a distance the famous battle-field of Kambula. We stayed the night at a kraal under Zunguin's hill, where they gave me a hut to myself.

10th.—Started early and passed all day through a desolated country. Nearly every kraal was deserted and not a sign of man was to be seen over many miles of country. These kraals belonged to the *Abaqulusi*, who were supposed to be under Oham; but they rebelled, and he sent an impi against them. A battle was fought on the banks of the Bivana river. The Abaqulusi were defeated and had to flee the country with their women, children, and cattle.

This happened a week ago. I crossed the river Bivana, and off-saddled at a kraal belonging to the big man of the district, Gedhlezi, where I was entertained as usual with amasi (milk curdled). I went on towards the Pongola river. Here the country became gradually dotted over with Boer's houses. I heard that there was a missionary on the other side of the Pongola, for whose house I made. As I crossed, I found that I was coming into a country occupied by the Boers. It is a strip,

---

* Here fell Colonel Wetherly, Piet Uys, &c.

partly Transvaal and partly a country over-run by the Dutch, which intervenes between Zululand and Swaziland, N. I rode up to the missionary's house, and asked for a night's lodging. He seemed to be a German, and looked much surprised to see me. He called his wife to interpret. She came and said they were very sorry, but they dared not put me up even for the night, for war had broken out again between the Dutch and English, and that no Englishman would be allowed in the country. She advised me to turn back into Zululand at once. Her arguments were seconded by those of a Boer, who said that I should be turned back by force. I declined the offer of a cup of coffee, and turning my horse's head, rode slowly back and recrossed the river, much to the wonder of Inkuna. We stayed the night at a kraal of the Amaswazi near the river.

11*th.*—Started early and rode straight back to Gedhlezi's kraal, hoping to discover a road in Swaziland by crossing the river lower down; but I could not hear of any such road, and so turned towards home.

Soon after crossing the river Bivana, your poor old horse, "Dean," knocked up, and I was forced to leave him. After going three miles we came to

a kraal where there was an old couple, who had
been left behind, on the flight of the Abaqulusi
(*ukulinda umuzi*), to take care of the kraal.   The
old man was too feeble to be moved.   The old
woman would have pleased you; she was the nicest
old Kafir woman I have ever come across.   She
seemed quite pleased to see us, and gave us some
maize to cook (as she could not fetch water for
herself), and a hut to sleep in.   We fed on boiled
maize, and lay down to sleep.

12*th.*—When we found the old horse he was
feeding quietly.   Inkuna led him gently all that
day.   We reached the kraal of Inkosana that night,
and slept there.   He was one of Ketchwayo's chief
indunas, and went with him to the Cape; he has
come back to see his people, but is going to return
to the Cape.   He showed me photos of Ketchwayo
and his induna, and also of Captain Pool.   Whilst
I was there, some of the Abaqulusi, who were
staying the night at a kraal on their way to
Mr. Osborne's (the British Resident) at Inhlazatshe,
were giving a description of the recent battle with
Oham, in which they had taken part.   They said
that four white men were with Oham's impi
(army); they also described some horrible barbarities
which had been committed by the victors after the

battle. I failed to obtain any cattle; all had some excuse for not selling.

13th.—At mid-day we halted at the chief kraal of Seketwayo (one of the thirteen chiefs), whose district adjoins Hlubi's. I found the chief a fat, uncomfortable-looking old man, with no voice; he was sitting in his hut, surrounded by his indunas (headmen). He was anxious to hear all the news. He gave me the drink of utshwala (beer) out of his own kamba (bowl), which ordinary politeness enjoined to a distinguished visitor. I stayed two or three hours, and then went on.

Towards evening the old horse knocked up. We stayed the night at a kraal, where the people treated us very well, though the Umninimuzana was only an Umfokazana.

There is a great difference in the way they treat one. Of course, when you ask for anything, they invariably say that you have come at a time of famine, when they have positively nothing to eat. This is always the native way of speaking; but, after that, they seem to try all they can to make you comfortable, and bring you all the delicacies they have. Others only give because they think they must.

14th.—Found the old horse quite dead. I took

him over 200 miles in that week. This is the fourth horse they have lost. One of the natives was struck by lightning yesterday, and killed on the spot.

30th.—Sihhayo, deposed chief of this district, has been here. He came to Church and, with Hlubi, looked at a map of the territories, drank sugar and water, and talked. It was strange to see the old chief and the new one on such good terms. He wishes to be allowed to settle again here. He is a fine-looking old fellow, tall and stout.

November 11th.—I have been to another hunt of quite a different style, held on the plain near the river. I shot two *pauws* (bustards), and ran down a buck with one of the Basuto; half fell to my share. I was in at the death on two other occasions. The plan is simply to run down the deer by hard galloping.

Charles is quite well again. Our hours are:—Up at 6; prayers, 7.30; breakfast, after school, 11; dinner, 1.30; school, 3 P.M.; tea, 7 P.M.

27th.—We have had the honour of meeting General Sir Evelyn Wood to-day. About 4 P.M. Charles and I and Hlubi, and two of his men, started off to see him. We found the tents by Rorke's Drift. As we dismounted, Sir E. Wood came out of the tent, with General Buller, Major Fraser, and one or two others. We spent some time talking to them; a great deal of interpretation having to be done between the General and Hlubi, from whom he wanted three guides: one to take them to Isandhlwana, and thence to the Prince's grave, and so back. It will be over sixty miles, but they seem used to long distances. General Buller only left Maritzburg yesterday morning. General Wood inquired kindly after the Basuto by name. We reached home just in time to avoid a thunderstorm.

I went to the Ondini bush in John Dunn's district, the other day, to cut poles for the new stable roof (fifty miles). I got leave to cut from the man in charge. It is a grand country up there, very high. The views far down the valley of the Tugela, into Zululand on one side and Natal on the other, were magnificent. They reminded me of the Umkomazi valley from the top of Inkonya, only on a grander scale. The yellow-wood forests are like those which you have seen in Griqualand.

I was cutting for two days, and finished on Saturday, and loaded up in time to make one short trek by moonlight. Next day I left the waggon to rest (I had been sleeping under the waggon), and stayed at Isandhlwana all night. The waggon was days behind me, having been delayed by a stickfast and an upset.

December 1881.—On the 15th there was an extraordinary storm here. The wind was very high; the hailstones were as large as duck's eggs; some of them were as big as a man's fist. They came down with tremendous force, but happily not very close together. Gradually they got smaller and fell thicker, until they turned to heavy rain. Next morning Philemon appeared with a very long face and no waggon. The news he had to tell was very serious. The waggon had been washed down the river. They had stuck fast in the Umzinyatyana, a tributary of the Buffalo, which enters the river about three miles above Rorke's Drift. In ordinary weather it is only a little stream, but when the storm came on the river came down with a rush. They had only just time to unhook the oxen and get them out before the *wave* was upon them. The waggon was carried over and down stream as though it had been a piece of wood, and not a heavy buck waggon with three tons load on it. On hearing of our misfortune, we set off to save what we could out of the wreck. We went straight to the hut by the river-side, viz., Charles, Mr. May,

and his brother and myself, and the German who
had been building the stable here, with a waggon
and all the natives we have at work on the place
(twenty-five). We went straight to the hut by
the river, where we have two boys. We found
that they had been busy since daylight and had
rescued several boxes and things which had been
floating down the river or had got stranded on the
rocks. Very fortunately, the Buffalo river had not
been affected by the storm, and was quite low;
otherwise everything which had reached the main
stream must have been carried down entirely out
of our reach. We tried to launch the boat, but it
leaked and nearly went to the bottom. We then
crossed the river and made our way to the place
where the accident had happened. All the way up
we found boxes and things which had been stranded
or fished out. When we reached the waggon itself,
we found it even worse than we expected. It was
a complete wreck ; the buck was about 200 yards
below the place where the waggon stuck, half-
buried in the sand, with nothing left in it but some
roofing iron of Mr. May's. On the top of the buck
and standing right across it were the two hind
wheels complete, with part of the understill. The
buck was very much broken and the iron of it

twisted, and so with the rest of the waggon. One of the fore-wheels had every spoke smashed, and the ring of the felloes bound by the tire was found at a long way from the nave, which was still on the axle. The force of the water must have been terrific. One thick iron crowbar was bent nearly double, while some of the irons of the waggon were bent and broken as though they had been so much wire. We spent the whole day getting out the wreckage and recovering such goods as we could find, about half the load in bulk, but not nearly half in value, as some of the things were quite ruined and nearly all of them much damaged. Some of the things were fished out about three miles down the river. Our loss, including the waggon, which was a hired one, nearly new, worth £120, cannot be much less than £150, while Mr. May's is reckoned at £200.

Jan. 28th, 1882.—We have been honoured by a visit from His Excellency the Administrator, Colonel Mitchell, who came to visit the field of battle. Hlubi called his people together, 200 Basuto mounted, and nearly a thousand Zulus on foot. The Zulus were a curious mixture as regards costume, some being dressed in full Zulu war-dress, with magnificent plumes and tails, while many had a sort of compromise, being adorned like the Natal natives, some with a waistcoat, some with a shirt, some with a coat or a hat; but the most incongruous thing, when the whole body was on the trot, chanting as they went, was to see two or three umbrellas, striped white, red, blue, green, and yellow, bobbing up and down amongst them. The Basuto go through the ordinary cavalry movements very fairly, and obey the word of command readily. We met Colonel Mitchell close to Isandhlwana with Mr. Fynn (magistrate at Umsinga) and two or three other gentlemen who had come up with him. An interchange of civilities followed. Hlubi drew up his men and gave three cheers. We then rode with Colonel Mitchell as far as the drift, escorted by Hlubi's troop. He was going to Helpmakaar for the night. At the boat we took our leave of him and rode home. The other day a pigeon, which was pursued by a hawk, flew into this room, where it was caught by the boys.

January 12th.—Having told you of our great misfortune, I will now tell you of our pleasant journey to Maritzburg. We started last Wednesday in a nice carriage belonging to a native. It seats four and has a hood. We took with us a little boy of the owner, a tiny boy, but very sharp and clever

with the harness, and Untombi, one of our girls.
It is a great treat for her. She is astonished at all
she sees. We stayed over Thursday at Mr. Dill's,
and went on on Friday, dining at Helpmakaar, a
nice clean little hotel. Indeed, we were surprised
how neat and clean the inns were all along the road.
After dinner we went on to Umsinga, and slept at
Sandspruit, a bright little inn two miles beyond.
On Saturday we reached Tugela river by mid-
day, and dined there. There is a new punt, like
a floating bridge, large enough for a waggon with
four oxen to drive on. We sat in the carriage
as we crossed, and simply drove on and off. At
night we reached Mooi river, a pretty place down
in the thorns, with plenty of trees in the garden.
Here we stayed till Sunday evening, and then went
on. We drove through the river. One of the
horses refused to go on in the middle, and in consequence the bar to which the traces are fastened
was broken, and we had to get some men to push
at the wheels before we could get the horse to
move. We went up and up through the thorns,
and slept at Burrup's, a nice place on the top. The
proprietor is an Oxford man; a come-down for him
to be keeping an hotel. It used to be a canteen,
but he has given that up. You can see at once

that he is an educated man. You cannot think what a treat the fruit, fresh meat, and change of food altogether is to us. At midday on Monday we reached Greytown, and dined at the Handleys', some people whom Charles knows. They have a magnificent place; plantations of gum-trees (eucalyptus) stretch a long distance on each side. Then there is a beautiful garden, and the house is just like a lovely English one, full of every comfort and luxury, and very large. It was luxurious to sit in that beautiful drawing-room, with cool verandah, shaded with creepers, and the light softened with plants and flowers and Venetian blinds. We stopped the night at Sevenoaks, the only uncomfortable place we stayed at. The next place was Sterkspruit, pretty, with plenty of trees and flowers; and on to Umgeni in the afternoon, where there is a beautiful hotel with every comfort. There are lovely waterfalls to be seen from the broad verandah, which goes nearly round the house. Wednesday turned out very wet, so we stayed all day, and on Thursday morning came on to Maritzburg (a week after leaving home).

APPENDIX.

COPY of a LETTER dated the 3rd of May 1882, Isandhlwana, Zululand:—

ZULULAND is gradually but surely drifting into a state of anarchy. I will now try to explain the state of affairs. The country is divided into three factions:—

1st. Those who wish the English Government to take them under its protection, and put them on a footing with the natives of Natal, *i.e.* each native to be under his own hereditary chief, subject to resident European magistrates, who would all be under the British Resident, who would collect the taxes for the Queen. They all talk of taxes being collected and sent to the Queen. This faction is by far the largest of the three. It takes in nine of the thirteen chiefs, and nearly all the Zulu people.

2nd. The King's party, *i.e.* all those who look
forward to Ketchwayo's return, or, in default of
that, who wish his brother Undabuko to be made
Regent, until the King's son, now fifteen years old,
should grow up. This faction is a very large one
also, because many of those who belong to No. 1
say, " If we cannot get English rule, let us have
our own king back again."

3rd. Followers and friends of John Dunn, a
small minority, but strong, because they are in
possession. Dunn's party is composed of his own
clan, Oham and his clan, and Usibepu and his clan.
By "clan" I do not mean all the people of their
districts, for their own clans form but a small
portion of them. This third faction is opposed to
the other two ; they want neither European
protection, nor Ketchwayo's return.

I have not classed the Chief Hlubi with any of
these. He stands alone ready to obey the commands of the Governor of Natal, as represented by
Mr. Osborne, the British Resident. Sir H. Bulwer
is High Commissioner of Zululand, and represents
the Queen.

Hlubi (with his Basuto) is ready to do what he
is ordered. He does not want to fight, but he will
defend himself if attacked; but one half of the

Zulus under him would join Undabuko—the head of the King's party—if it came to a trial of strength.

Now for the reason of all this discontent and disturbance.

Before Chaka became Chief, what is now Zululand was then shared by a number of small tribes. Chaka overcame all these tribes; some of them were larger than his own. He did not break them up—nor are they yet broken up—but are as distinct now as they were in the time of Zenzangakona. But then each chief looked to Chaka and his successors, viz. Dingaan, Panda, Ketchwayo, as their chief paramount. Now had the Commissioners who divided Zululand after the late war taken the clannish feeling into consideration, and divided it as it was in the time of Chaka's father, allowing each clan to be governed by its own chief or induna, with a British Resident to appeal to, Zululand would have been as quiet to-day as anyone could wish. Instead of that, Zululand was divided into thirteen portions, regardless of clan or tribe. The old clans were divided, and placed under alien chiefs, indunas of other clans, who have been raised to the rank of petty kings. Hence all this trouble. Each clan still looks to its own chief, although, according to the present settlement, he is no chief at all. This irritates the Chiefs placed in office by the Commission, and some of them try to enforce obedience and recognition: *e.g.* Oham has under him, besides his own clan, part of the Amaqulusi tribe; but they hate him, and consider themselves, as a tribe, superior to Oham's clan. Of course they felt aggrieved at being placed under him, and have never recognised him. So, whenever any case was brought before Oham for judgment by an outsider against the Amaqulusi, they would not abide by his decision. This produced an open rupture. Oham soon found a pretext for using force. Watching his opportunity, he fell upon the Amaqulusi, and slaughtered all he could lay hands on, " eating up" everything he could find. The Amaqulusi, a powerful and warlike tribe, assembled themselves from all parts, and were preparing to attack Oham in force to avenge their fallen brothers, when Mr. Osborne very bravely went to the place of muster, and managed to make them disperse to their kraals. This is but one instance. I could fill volumes with the same kind of matter; but this is enough to show what I mean. The Commissioners entirely misunderstood the nature of the Zulus. Simple as he is, the Zulu is not a baby; but he is really a very reasonable being, with strong convictions and very conservative ideas, rarely asserting himself or putting forward his opinion in opposition to those in authority, patient and enduring under lawful authority, but when roused he is as obstinate as a mule, and straight to his object he rushes like " a bull at a gate." Were these the people that the Commission thought to bind down to a mushroom system, trampling under foot habits and feelings as strong as the hills, by simply going through the land and mapping it out, thus breaking up hereditary tribes, and transferring their allegiance by a stroke of the pen! What blindness! Chaka, savage as he was, showed far wiser statecraft. He, after conquering the clans, bound them to himself, yet left each under its own chief. The natives are like the Highlanders, very clannish. Outrage this feeling and you have discontent and rebellion.

Those who placed these chiefs in their present position, are more to blame than the chiefs themselves. A man suddenly finds himself placed over chiefs and clans who, a few months ago, were his equals or superiors—men like Undabuko, Umnyamana, Dabulamanzi—whom he had to obey in fear and trembling. What wonder that now he should show his power, and enrich himself at their expense? When the same man who exacts fines is the one to benefit by the fines, what wonder if he should be quick at looking up cases? This irritates the people; they show it, and then they are fined the more, until they rebel, and then they are "eaten up."

When this "eating up" took place in the olden time, if the man managed to escape, no thought of rebellion entered his head, because he knew he was always liable to it, and he considered that the King had a right to do what he liked. But when they were conquered by the English, having heard so much of the freedom of the Natal natives, and the safety of their property, the Zulus naturally expected that " eating up " had passed away with the old *régime*. This expectation greatly tended at first to do away with the bitter feeling that they felt at having been conquered and deprived of their king.

Again, when taxes were first levied, the people thought the money would go to the High Commissioner, or the Crown; but now that they see that each Chief collects for himself, the irritation is increased.

Again, in the case of secreting the King's cattle,

or being suspected of having hidden away plunder from the battle-fields, what wonder that a chief should be eager in hunting out and "eating up" all the suspected ones ?

This is clutched at as being a splendid legal way of eating up a man, and sometimes even a whole clan.

There is not one native in Zululand who thinks that the present settlement is righteous. Of one chief the natives say :—" He was a little dog, found by the King; he was cold, so the King put him by his fire to get warm. Now he has driven the King from his fire, his hearth, and has taken possession of it; but he is still only a dog."

Again the Zulus complain that the English have conquered them, have taken away their King for their good, it was said. They were told that all oppression and arbitrary government would be done away with. But instead of being taken under the protection of the English, they have been simply thrown over and delivered up to be oppressed and plundered by people who have no right over them, either by hereditary authority or conquest. They are bound down to this rule, and are not allowed to have a voice in the matter.

There are two ways in which this state of

anarchy could be put an end to without bloodshed, first, by annexation, and, secondly, by the return of Ketchwayo; but whether the settlement would then be permanent it is impossible to say.   There is no doubt but that the whole of Zululand, except J. Dunn, Oham, and Usibepu, would gladly welcome annexation in this way, each clan to be under its own head, with powers as enjoyed by the chiefs in Natal, subject to resident magistrates, who should be controlled by a chief magistrate. The whole should be under the Governor of Natal as High Commissioner and Supreme Chief of the natives, assisted and advised by the Natal House of Assembly.   It would not be a burden to Natal, for the revenue would pay all expenses and leave a surplus, which could be expended on public works. Annexation is what the people are clamouring for. If they cannot get this, they ask that Ketchwayo may be brought back and allowed to govern, being *publicly replaced*.   If he were merely *allowed* to return, there would be opposition, fighting, and bloodshed.   Unless replaced by the English, the people would be afraid to join him for fear o displeasing the " Abelungu " (white men).

Extract from a Letter from G. Ll. Jenkinson,
  dated 8th June 1882, from Zululand, near
  Rorke's Drift:—

Things in Zululand are fast coming to a crisis.
Since Sir H. Bulwer turned back that deputation,
and Undabuko and the rest of the chiefs returned
to Zululand, it has been pretty certain that serious
disturbances must break out very shortly, and now
I am afraid it has actually begun.

Our chief, Hlubi, went some few days ago up
to Inhlazatshe to see Mr. Osborne (British Resident).
He has just come back, and gives a very bad account
of the state of the whole country. Everyone is up
in arms. It is reported that an engagement has
taken place. The immediate occasion of all this is
the way in which that deputation which went down
to Maritzburg was treated. If the Governor had
listened to their grievances, or even told them that
these would be inquired into at the proper time,
they would have gone back and waited, trusting
that something would be done ; but, instead
of that, they were told to go back to their own
chiefs, that the Governor would have nothing to say
to them; they had chiefs of their own and must

obey them. The object of the deputation was, that the country might be taken under British rule, or else that Ketchwayo might be restored. They could not endure the present state of things or submit any longer to the rule of the " Abafokazana " (*i.e.* " strangers," used contemptuously of the chiefs).

As soon as they returned from Pietermaritzburg, Undabuko, the ex-king's brother, who was one of the chief movers in the matter, began organising his army, as also did the famous Umnyamana (who commanded at Kambula and was prime minister). They purpose overthrowing all the present chiefs and setting up again a united kingdom. From nearly every chief in Zululand numbers have gone to join their ranks. Some chiefs have lost all their tribe except their own personal followers. From John Dunn, however, only one chief has gone, Dabulamanzi, although thirteen out of sixteen who formed the deputation to Pietermaritzburg came out of his district. The plan arranged by the insurgents, if such they can be called, is rather bold and sweeping. First, it is said, they intend to divide their forces, Umnyamana going against Oham, whilst Undabuko makes for Usibepu. When they have polished off these two, they intend

to join together and attack John Dunn. When he
is disposed of, they are going to make short work
of Hlubi and his lot. This is said to be their
programme, but whether they will be able to carry
it out or not remains to be seen. They will find
Oham and Usibepu rather rough customers to
begin with, as all their people are with them.
Mr. Osborne, B.R., seems to be in a queer fix.
He says he can do nothing, poor man. He has
now left Inhlazatshe. To-day a runner arrived
from him with despatches for the Government of
Natal, asking Hlubi to forward them at once to the
Umsinga. Hlubi instantly despatched a mounted
man to carry them there.

You must have heard something of the state
of the country, long ere you receive this, from tele-
grams. These often give a wrong impression,
unless the news be of a very defined character,
such as that a battle was fought, &c. Of course
you must not take all this as exactly true. The
details may be wrong and mixed up, as native
reports often are ; but this is certain, that a great
part of Zululand is in arms. I am glad that we
are in this particular part of Zululand amongst the
Basuto. This is the only district (south-west, by
Rorke's Drift and Isandhlwana) in which there has

been no disturbance. I don't mean to say that it has been by any means *perfectly* governed, but it has been better than the others. Hlubi would make a good fight for it if attacked. The Zulus in the district, though quiet and contented at present, having no desire to fight, would, I think, if it came to the point whether they would fight for Hlubi or Undabuko, decide in favour of Umtwana ka Umpande (Panda's child).

P.S.—I have very little to add to my contribution to South African history. I have tried to present a faithful and true picture of the country as it has come under my notice and under the notice of my children. I believe that the British rule has been, on the whole, a blessing to the country, spite of blemishes, and I hope and pray that this rule may be continued without destroying the system of governing the natives through their own hereditary chiefs.

NOTE.

As I have been often asked to pronounce the name of the captive Chief now daily expected in England, I may say that the first half is pronounced as I have spelt it—" Ketch "—only there is an initial click signified by the letter C. The latter part is pronounced very broad, something like " wyeo."

Bishop Colenso spells it Cetywayo, according to the derivation, I suppose, as I take it to be a verbal pass. participle of " ceba," to devise. The Zulus often call their children after some passing event or circumstance. I have never heard the reason why such a name was given to the son of Umpande.

The " ty " is pronounced almost like " ch," so Tyaka is the same as Chaka, the " a " always being full and broad like the Italian; and so Ketchwāyo comes nearest in English.